Issues in Historiography

The debate on the decline of Spain

D1642908

MANCHESTER
1824

Manchester University Press

Issues in Historiography
General editor
R. C. RICHARDSON
University of Winchester

Already published

The Debate on the Norman Conquest
Marjorie Chibnall

The Debate on the French Revolution
Peter Davies

Debates on the Holocaust
Tom Lawson

The Debate on the American Revolution
Gwenda Morgan

The Debate on the English Revolution
R. C. Richardson

The Debate on the American Civil War Era
H. A. Tulloch

The Debate on the Crusades
Christopher Tyerman

The Debate on Black Civil Rights in America
Kevern Verney

The Debate on the Rise of the British Empire
Anthony Webster

Issues in Historiography

The debate on the decline of Spain

HELEN RAWLINGS

MANCHESTER
UNIVERSITY PRESS
MANCHESTER AND NEW YORK

distributed in the United States exclusively by Palgrave Macmillan

Published by Manchester University Press
Oxford Road, Manchester M13 9NR, UK
and Room 400, 175 Fifth Avenue, New York, NY 10010, USA
www.manchesteruniversitypress.co.uk

Distributed in the United States exclusively by
Palgrave Macmillan, 175 Fifth Avenue, New York,
NY 10010, USA

Distributed in Canada exclusively by
UBC Press, University of British Columbia, 2029 West Mall,
Vancouver, BC, Canada V6T 1Z2

British Library Cataloguing-in-Publication Data
A catalogue record for this book is available from the British Library

Library of Congress Cataloging-in-Publication Data applied for

ISBN   978 0 7190 7963 4 hardback

ISBN   978 0 7190 7964 1 paperback

First published 2012

Typeset
by Action Publishing Technology Ltd, Gloucester
Printed in Great Britain
by Bell & Bain Ltd, Glasgow

For my mother

CONTENTS

FIGURES

GENERAL EDITOR'S FOREWORD

History without historiography is a contradiction in terms. The study of the past cannot be separated from the linked study of its practitioners and intermediaries. No historian writes in isolation from the work of his or her predecessors, nor can the commentator – however clinically objective or professional – stand aloof from the insistent pressures, priorities and demands of the ever-changing present. In truth there are no self-contained academic 'ivory towers'. Historians' writings are an extension of who they are and where they are placed. Though historians address the past as their subject they always do so in ways that are shaped – consciously or unconsciously as the case may be – by the society, cultural ethos, politics and systems of their own day, and they communicate their findings in ways which are specifically intelligible and relevant to a reading public consisting initially of their own contemporaries. For these reasons the study of history is concerned most fundamentally not with dead facts and sterile, permanent verdicts but with highly charged dialogues, disagreements, controversies and shifting centres of interest among its presenters, with the changing methodologies and discourse of the subject over time, and with audience reception. *Issues in Historiography* is a series designed to explore such matters by means of case studies of key moments in world history and the interpretations, reinterpretations, debates and disagreements they have engendered.

Helen Rawlings' book exemplifies this agenda very clearly and fits neatly into the series. It also fills a notable gap in the available literature. The decline of Spain has been much studied as a historical subject in ways which have emphasised the effects of imperial over-extension, warfare, plague, inflation and taxation. The historiography of the subject, by contrast, has up to now rarely received the proper attention which it merits. Rawlings guides her readers sequentially through a complex multi-layered subject, making clear how many of the dominant paradigms of Spanish decline were constructed and imposed by grossly biased outsiders. Above all, the 'Black Legend', highlighting the stifling effects on Spain of the Inquisition, was created and fuelled in the sixteenth and seventeenth centuries by that country's Protestant enemies in northern Europe. In the later eighteenth century, French writers such as Voltaire, looking down from the lofty heights of the Enlightenment, arrogantly dismissed Spain in the early modern period as despotic, intolerant and decadent. American writers of the nineteenth century, Motley and Prescott among them, had other axes to grind. With the exception of the *arbitristas* of the early modern period, the much later Generation of '98 which spoke out after Spain's loss of its last Central American territories at the very end of the nineteenth century, and from the 1950s the Barcelona School, the Spanish historical academy itself remained backward, inward looking and unheard in the wider world. Rather notably, Spain's home-grown historiography of the early modern decline of the country did not really begin to flourish until after the end of the Franco regime in 1975. Now, after a very delayed start, Spain's own historians are taking a lead in asking new questions, establishing a new quantitative dimension to the subject and exploring all manner of regional complexities. Outsiders like John Elliott and Henry Kamen have now been joined by a new generation of Spain's own historians. For them, re-examining a critical phase of Spain's past has been bound up with the redefinition and relaunching of Spain in the present.

All this, and more, Rawlings makes clear in a compact and tautly argued study which will surely help students to negotiate this difficult subject and assist them to unpack the baggage of past and present commentators who have been drawn to it. Moreover, as present-day Spain attempts to confront its current insistent economic crisis as this book goes to press, it is surely timely to review interpretations of that country's epic time of malfunctioning in the past.

R.C. Richardson
September 2011

PREFACE

The decline of Spain figures as a major, recurring theme in any study of Spanish history and has given rise to a vigorous exchange of ideas and regular rereading of the complex circumstances that prompted the phenomenon by successive generations of international historians. However, the ensuing debate and the voluminous amount of scholarship it has inspired have not hitherto been approached from a historiographical perspective. The present book aims to bridge that gap and to contribute to other historiographical case studies of major debates in world history covered in the *Issues in Historiography* series. It is designed to serve as background to how the debate on Spain's decline has evolved over the centuries via the historians who have participated in it, the influences that have shaped their outlook on events and the trends in historical research and discourse that have informed it. It presupposes some prior knowledge while encouraging further study. It is built on the premise that it is through an appreciation of the construction and evolution of history that a better understanding of the historical phenomenon itself becomes possible. The book is a product of my own learning, teaching, research and writing in the field of early modern Spanish history over many years, inspired and challenged by some of the eminent historians who have given rise to the debate and whose work is discussed here. It stands as testimony of their efforts to make sense of the past above my own. I wish to extend my thanks to Professor Roger Richardson, the Series Editor, for his guidance, and the production team at Manchester University Press for their assistance. I also wish to acknowledge my gratitude to the Scouloudi Foundation, in association with the Institute of Historical Research, University of London, for the award of a grant which facilitated the research for this project, as well as to the University of Leicester for the period of study leave which enabled me to complete the writing.

INTRODUCTION

Historians are bound by right to be exact, truthful, and absolutely unprejudiced, so that neither interest nor fear, dislike nor affection, should make them turn from the path of truth, whose mother is history, rival of time, storehouse of great deeds, witness of the past, example and lesson to the present, warning to the future. (Miguel de Cervantes, *The Adventures of Don Quixote* [1605], trans. J.M. Cohen [Harmondsworth, 1973], Part I, Chap. IX, p. 78)

Since the beginning of the seventeenth century, when Cervantes' Don Quixote uttered these immortal words, writers reflecting on Spain's past history have traditionally accounted for its development in the early modern period in terms of its rise and decline. According to the standard narrative interpretation, later adopted by historians, in the course of the sixteenth century Spain underwent a remarkable transformation in its history. From being a weak, fragmented country with a large rural population and little natural wealth, it became united under strong monarchical leadership and grew in demographic strength and productivity. It colonized a vast overseas empire, rich in gold and silver, developed organs of government to administer law and order throughout its territories, and rose to become the wealthiest and most powerful nation-state in Christendom. From the last decades of the sixteenth century onwards, however, Spain's economic fortunes went into steady recession, while the effects of plague, the heavy cost of warfare and crippling levels of taxation severely weakened society. By 1650, the Spanish monarchy could no longer sustain its leading role on the world stage and thereafter was reduced to the status of a second-rate European power.[1]

The circumstances surrounding the collapse of Spain from the dominant position it held for much of the sixteenth century in terms of the power and influence it wielded, to that of a state which by the middle of the seventeenth century had suffered a dramatic reversal of its political and economic fortunes, has generated one of the most seminal 'rise and decline' debates in early

1

modern history, which continues to exercise the minds of some of the most influential scholars of Spanish history to this day. The fundamental question of why Spain fell into decline as a nation has, over the course of the centuries, been informed by historical myth and legend; subject to competing ideologies, schools and prejudices among historians; analysed from different theoretical and methodological standpoints; as well as being conditioned by the unfolding events of history itself. As a result, the decline thesis has frequently been contested, adapted, revised and even overturned altogether by successive generations of historians.

The problem of decline has not only shaped the debate itself but also defined the long view of Spain's historical trajectory. By building upon preconceived judgements of its predisposition for greatness and failure, historians have tended to identify the ongoing fluctuations in its fortunes as a continuum of past events. While the phenomenon of decline had become a common denominator of its history, the historiographical trends that have shaped the discourse – essentially 'borrowed' from other nations – have not been studied or theorized in any great depth. This may be partly due to the lack of recognition given to the discipline of historiography in Spain itself until the twentieth century. Native Catholic historians have long argued a case for Spain to be considered as different from other European countries in terms of its historical development and therefore not subject to the same criteria by which they have been judged. This self-imposed isolationism from historical trends, coupled with its own political marginalization from Europe, resulted in the stagnation of historical studies in Spain for much of the nineteenth and early twentieth centuries and in its history being 'taken over' by foreign historians (principally French, British and American) who, from the 1950s, took the lead in removing it from its strait jacket and forging innovative research. Many of its major historians are still unknown outside Spain today and their research inaccessible to other scholars, other than Hispanists. Rarely do they figure in historiographical or bibliographical surveys.[2] It is only in recent decades that this imbalance has begun to be addressed.

On account of these circumstances, any attempt to label historians – especially those of native origin – who have contributed to the debate according to the school of history to which they belong is beset with difficulties, at least until the middle of the twentieth century, when theoretical fields of enquiry first began to infiltrate the discourse. Of much greater relevance to understanding the course that the history of decline has taken is the political, religious and intellectual standpoint of its contributors. Two fundamental and diametrically opposed 'black and white' hypotheses have driven the debate since its inception (sometimes referred to as the 'Two Spains' conundrum), informed on either side by the ideologies of Catholicism and Protestantism, the politics of conservatism and liberalism, the philosophies of traditionalism and rationalism and the economic principles of mercantilism and free trade. Socialist and capitalist interpretations have made less impact on the debate, due to the fact that the industrial and social revolutions that prompted them barely touched Spain. Likewise, historians who have attempted to examine decline via a deconstruction of the Old Regime have found discrepancies in the model when applied to Spain, while postmodern trends in research have barely made their mark on the discourse. Thus the debate has developed along lines determined largely by historical forces rather than by schools or theories. Despite the polarization of viewpoints that have informed the historiography, a surprising consensus of opinion has emerged in certain key areas, as this study will show.

The development of historical studies as a discipline in Spain has also influenced the way the discourse has evolved. One of the arguments put forward by eighteenth-century Spanish scholars such as Juan Pablo Forner was that the history of their decline as a nation had largely been written by foreigners who denigrated their reputation via a series of false accusations which they had failed to refute, thereby allowing a fabricated version of events to circulate. Despite attempts to professionalize the field and adopt the new scientific methods of enquiry being pursued by European historians, in the nineteenth century what constituted 'history' in Spain was largely polemical and persuasive, conditioned by the partisanship of writers rather than their critical examination of original evidence. History books in the main comprised collections of documents or general histories of Spain that followed a narrative tradition in which the Church and monarchy figured prominently. Spanish national archives were poorly catalogued and their resources tended to be exploited primarily by foreign historians. Although the value of history as a tool of learning and self-improvement was becoming recognized by native historians at the beginning of the twentieth century, it was not until the aftermath of the Civil War in the 1950s and the emergence of the academic historian in Spain that the discourse gradually began to evolve along impartial lines. This had important repercussions for the decline debate, which became more open to self-criticism and foreign intervention as a consequence. Even so, liberal-minded historians had to steer a careful course so as not to offend the right-wing regime which controlled the agenda and funding of historical research. Some leading intellectuals were forced into exile to express their views.[3] By contrast, in post-Franco Spain, the study of history, consistent with the country's new political orientation, has become 'democratized' and valued as an important means of reconciliation with the past, forging revisionist interpretations of its decline.

The aim of this book is to address the decline of Spain as a historiographical as opposed to a historical phenomenon and to bring its study into the framework of other great historical debates covered in this series that have shaped history through the ages. It will trace the evolution of the discourse that has informed the debate from the sixteenth century to the present day, identifying the main contributors and the influences that have defined their outlook. It will consider why the subject has provoked such a controversial and prolonged exchange among historians and the ways in which they have attempted to explain the circumstances that gave rise to Spain's decline and its consequences. It will compare and contrast their different interpretations and link their ideas and methods of enquiry to both the historical and historiographical contexts in which they wrote, using extracts from their work to illustrate their approaches. It will thus contribute to our understanding of both the makers and the making of one of the defining periods in Spain's history.

In the sixteenth century, as Chapter 1 will illustrate, Spain's Protestant enemies were responsible for the propagation of the so-called 'Black Legend', which subsequently became the blueprint of the decline thesis for those of liberal persuasion for generations to come. It was formulated not by historians but by polemicists, such as the Spanish Protestant exile Gonsalvius Montanus and leader of the Dutch Revolt William of Orange, whose aim was to denigrate Spain via a series of exaggerated indictments linked to its character and religious policies. According to the precepts of the Black Legend, Spain's decay as a nation was embodied in the oppressive machinery of the Inquisition, which cut it off from progress and stunted its growth, while its rigid, messianic adherence to the defence of Catholicism led it to commit barbarous atrocities and engage in coercive, rapacious imperialism. The conservative tradition subsequently became embodied in the counterpart 'White Legend', which emphasized the orthodox values and spirit intrinsic to Spain's rise to greatness and held anti-Catholic influences responsible for undermining its achievement and bringing about its demise. Its proponents fiercely defended Spain's exceptional, providential role in history as its major strength which set it apart from other nations. Neither of these theories can be divorced from the myths and legends that sustained them.[4]

While the issue of religion played a key part in the sixteenth-century debate, in the seventeenth century economic theories on Spain's fortunes abounded, penned by contemporary Spanish commentators known as *arbitristas*, who were the first writers to use the term 'decline' in their discourse and whose work will form the focus of Chapter 2. They saw themselves acting in an advisory capacity to the king and government and competed with one another to find solutions to the problems Spain faced. Although they tended to originate from conservative backgrounds, they were essentially progressive in their judgements and helped to establish the science of political economy that later generations of historians would develop. They were at one in pointing to the dissipation of New World wealth and the pursuit of mercantilist policies as the principal cause of their nation's ruin.

The eighteenth century witnessed the emergence of philosophical approaches to Spain's decline, inspired by the Enlightenment. French writers and philosophers in particular, including Montesquieu and Voltaire, were responsible for forging vitriolic attacks on Spain's cultural and intellectual backwardness, reviving the Black Legend by attributing its decadence to the despotism and intolerance associated with the practices of the Spanish Inquisition, together with an unwillingness to embrace the change and progress ushered in by the Age of Reason. These views, explored in Chapter 3, were counterbalanced by the emergence of liberal Spanish economists from within the administration of Charles III who put forward a series of pragmatic solutions to revive Spain's prosperity, drawn from their engagement with enlightened views and the rise of industrialization elsewhere in Europe. Although history had not yet fully emerged as a field of enquiry, its practical value in refuting 'foreign exaggerations' was acknowledged.

The nineteenth century, addressed in Chapter 4, marked a significant turning point in both the theoretical and practical orientation of decline discourse. As historical studies developed as a professional discipline, underpinned by evidence as opposed to bias, so it opened up the hitherto 'black' and 'white' nature of the debate to critical, objective analysis. Native Spanish history, however, set against the backdrop of political turmoil between liberals and conservatives, responded slowly to these developments and, despite some advances, essentially remained polarized in its outlook and didactic in its objectives until the end of the century. Meanwhile the debate continued to engage foreign scholars, including the American William Prescott, whose work reflected the nationalist sensitivities that characterized the age, and his compatriot Henry Charles Lea, who began to forge a 'middle way' through the discourse.

The relinquishing of Spain's last overseas possessions in Central America and the Pacific in 1898 provided a context for philosophical self-reflections on the question of imperialism in relation to decline on behalf of those intellectuals belonging to the so-called Generation of '98, such as José Ortega y Gasset and Miguel de Unamuno, whose writing is examined in Chapter 5. Like the *arbitristas* before them, they sought the means for national regeneration, either by embracing the traditional values that underpinned Spain's imperial past or by rejecting them in favour of a modern European agenda, reflecting in their views the nationalist and republican political divide of early twentieth-century Spain on the eve of the Spanish Civil War. At the same time professional historians, including Rafael Altamira and Ramón Menéndez Pidal, began to address the subject from non-partisan perspectives, in accordance with modern historiographical trends.

The revolutionary new approaches and methodologies that emerged from the French *Annales* School in the opening decades of the twentieth century, forged by Fernand Braudel among others, resulted in the application of the symptoms of Spain's decline to interdisciplinary theoretical analysis from the 1950s onwards. Chapter 6 shows how this allowed Spanish historians, led by Jaime Vicens Vives and his 'Barcelona School', to deconstruct the arguments from broader perspectives, including socio-economic fields, using 'long-run' evidence. The new historiography of decline inspired by these methods was non-biased and non-hierarchical in its scope, thus releasing the debate from the narrow political and ideological framework that had shaped its history over previous centuries. A further outcome was the dismantling of theories pertaining to the exceptional nature of Spain's historical trajectory to explain its rise and fall.

In the second half of the twentieth century a group of British historians, including the renowned Hispanist John Elliott, began to reconfigure the whole debate in the wider context of a seventeenth-century general European crisis rather than from the perspective of decline unique to Spain, using the journal *Past and Present* as a forum for lively debate. The political sympathies of the post-war generation found their voice in the theories of feudalism, capitalism and absolutism that underpinned the discourse. The comparative approach of the resulting historiography, explored in Chapter 7, allowed for these theories to be applied to Spain's own political and economic crisis and the extent of its convergence with the European model was subjected to rigorous analysis by a school of international historians.

More recently, Spain's transformation from dictatorship to democracy and the corresponding 'rediscovery' of its historical past has led to a fundamental revision of many of the old arguments and polarized judgements that have characterized Spanish decline historiography for centuries, conditioned by the prevailing political climate and the restrictions placed on native scholarship. Under the direction of a new generation of Spanish historians, the focus of the debate has fundamentally shifted from an examination of the socio-economic forces that underpinned the Old Regime to a consideration of the redistribution of power and resources that took place during the seventeenth century from the centre to peripheral regions and bodies, and that in turn gave way to recovery and survival. At the beginning of the twenty-first century, the issues that informed the debate on Spain's early modern crisis can be considered as a touchstone of its concerns in present-day times. These themes, addressed in Chapter 8, bring the book to its conclusion.

Although the discourse will be examined chronologically, it is possible to identify interdependence between the schools of thought that have fed the debate as historians have built upon each other's observations to formulate their views. Thus the theories of the *arbitrista* generation were revived by late eighteenth-century Spanish scholars to support a programme of economic recovery, while the Black Legend continued to be a reference point for liberal historians of decline well into the twentieth century. Finally, since historians, however impartial they might claim to be, have tended to use the preoccupations of their own times as departure points for their ideas, be they religious, philosophical, political or socio-economic, this has resulted in a study of the historiography of decline reflecting the forces that have shaped Spain's development through the centuries and not just those pertaining to the early modern period. So the decline question, and the strength of opinion that has informed the debate, continues to be relevant to how Spain, via its historians, has perceived itself at critical moments in its history, such as at the time of the Napoleonic invasions in 1808, following its collapse as a colonial power in 1898 and when the Civil War split it in two. This may account for its enduring fascination as a scholarly tradition and its value to those studying Spanish history today, as this book hopes to demonstrate.

Notes

1 General surveys of Spain's early modern history by British historians include: Martin. A.S. Hume, *The Court of Philip IV: Spain in Decadence* (London, 1928); R. Trevor Davies, *The Golden Century of Spain, 1501–1621* (London, 1937) and *Spain in Decline, 1621–1700* (London, 1957); J.H. Elliott, *Imperial Spain, 1469–1716* (Harmondsworth, 1970) and *The Count-Duke of Olivares. The Statesman in an Age of Decline* (New Haven, CT and London, 1986); John Lynch, *Spain 1516–1598: From Nation State to World Empire* (Oxford, 1991) and *The Hispanic World in Crisis and Change, 1598–1700* (Oxford, 1992); Henry Kamen, *Spain in the Later Seventeenth Century, 1665–1700* (London and New York, 1980) and *Spain, 1469–1714: A Society*

of Conflict (London and New York, 1983); James Casey, *Early Modern Spain: A Social History* (London and New York, 1999); Patrick Williams, *The Great Favourite. The Duke of Lerma and the Court and Government of Philip III of Spain, 1598–1621* (Manchester, 2006); Robert Stradling, *Philip IV and the Government of Spain, 1621–65* (Cambridge, 1998); Christopher Storrs, *The Resilience of the Spanish Monarchy, 1665–1700* (Oxford, 2007).

2 For example, the *Encyclopaedia of Historians and Historical Writing*, ed. Kelly Boyd (London, 1999) contains references to only three early modern Spanish historians under 'Spain and Portugal'.

3 See Gonzalo Pasamar, *Apologia and Criticism. Historical Writing in Spain 1500–2000* (Bern, 2010), chap. 4. Pasmar is currently the leading Spanish historian working in the field of historiography. In this excellent book, he examines its evolution through the theme of national identity.

4 J.N. Hillgarth, *The Mirror of Spain, 1500–1700. The Formation of a Myth* (Ann Arbor, MI, 2003) investigates how Spain was viewed by foreigners whose propaganda created a stereotypical image of its character and values.

1

The sixteenth century: the Black Legend

Oh wretched Spain! I have recalled a thousand times all your achievements and I have not found a single reason why you are worthy of such sustained persecution ... Who is there that does not regard us as mad, ignorant and proud, when all our vices come from abroad? (Francisco de Quevedo, *España Defendida* [1609], cited by Ricardo García Cárcel, *La Leyenda Negra. Historia y Opinión* [Madrid, 1998], p. 128)

What is the Black Legend? ... By the Black Legend we understand the reputation generated by the fictitious accounts about our land and people that have been widely circulated ... claiming that our country constitutes an unfortunate exception in the community of European nations in all that relates to toleration, culture and political progress. (Julián Juderías, *La Leyenda Negra: Estudios acerca del concepto de España en el Extranjero* [1914; reprinted, Madrid, 2007] pp. 13–14)

The Black Legend was a school of anti-Hispanic sentiment that grew up predominantly in northern European Protestant countries from the middle of the sixteenth century as a reaction against Spain's efforts to champion the cause of Catholicism via acts of aggressive imperialism abroad and exclusive religious and racial policies within its own shores. The Swedish historian Sverker Arnoldsson has suggested that it was a concept born in Italy, where Spaniards, as political and commercial rivals, were considered to exhibit the same characteristics as those attributed to the non-European groups with whom they shared a common ancestry.[1] Pope Paul IV (1556–59), in conflict with Philip II during his papacy, reportedly referred to them as 'heretics, schismatics,

11

accursed of God, the offspring of Jews and Marranos, the very scum of the earth'.[2] The English polemicist Edward Daunce reinforced this idea of racial impurity and inferiority in his *Brief Discourse of the Spanish State* (1590) by claiming that Spaniards were genealogically 'mingled with the Mores cruell and full of trecherie', stigmatizing Spain for its Moorish past despite its own self-styled image as the victorious power and civilization in the Christian Reconquest of the peninsula.[3] Spain's European enemies thus ruthlessly exploited its historic connections with Africa in order to underline its metaphorical 'blackness' and racial association with evil. While it was acknowledged by some contemporary writers that Spain had been elected to unite Christianity in the fight against the infidel and the heretic, it was understood that its role would be one of instructive leadership and not of tyrannical, imperialistic domination as perceived by her enemies. Accordingly, in the minds of rival nations, Spain became synonymous with all forms of repression, brutality, religious and racial intolerance, as well as intellectual and cultural backwardness that became embedded in the propagation of a powerful and uniquely black image which was to endure for centuries to come.[4]

The Legend has its written origins in several publications that circulated outside Spain at the end of the sixteenth century, some authored by exiled Spaniards and others by Protestant polemicists in northern Europe who vigorously promoted a negative impression of Spain via the power of the printing press. Their aim was to promulgate the blackest facts about Spain and its rulers to serve as a warning of the consequences of Spanish hegemony in Europe. The Spanish conquest of America and stories of the shameful treatment of native Amerindians by the conquistadors helped to advance the Legend. Bartolomé de Las Casas' *Brief Account of the Destruction of the Indies* (1552), in which the Dominican friar described with great passion the atrocities committed against innocent Indians and prophesized that such actions would lead to the conquering nation's own demise, was seized upon by Spain's enemies for their own political purposes. Likewise, the alleged brutality meted out by the Spanish Inquisition, circulated by Protestant pamphleteers, provided further evidence to support the Legend. One of the most influential of these was Reginaldus Gonsalvius Montanus, a member of the religious community of Seville who had fled Spain in 1557 along with other reform-minded individuals. In his *A Discovery and Plaine Declaration of sundry Subtill Practices of the Holy Inquisition of Spaine* (1567), he deliberately exaggerated the extent of the Inquisition's repressive practices for maximum effect. The wide dissemination of the text in several languages was to be a major factor that contributed to the persistence of anti-Spanish and anti-Inquisition propaganda in Protestant northern Europe for close on four centuries, influencing many polemical works, including the English perception of Spanish Catholicism elaborated by John Foxe in his *Acts and Monuments* (1563). Spain also became the target of an intense campaign of denigration on account of its religious policy in the Spanish Netherlands, led by one of the leaders of the Dutch Revolt, William of Orange, whose *Apology* of 1580 successfully stimulated aggressive Hispanophobia among fellow rebels. Black Legend literature continued to feed into the religious toleration debates of the following century, informing the *History of the Inquisition* (1692) by Philip van Limborch, an early participant in them. Overall, the influence of the Legend on the historiography of Spain's decline was unparalleled, to the extent that the debate might well not have acquired the intensity that it did without its precedence.

The writing of the Dominican friar Bartolomé de Las Casas (1474–1566), principal critic of the Spanish conquest and colonization of America, has acquired a special significance in the context of the development of the Black Legend and its relevance to the decline debate. In August 1514, after personally witnessing the oppression under which the native populations of Hispaniola and Cuba lived at the hands of Spanish settlers, he renounced his responsibilities as an *encomendero* (overlord of Indian community) and spent the remaining fifty years of his life passionately defending their rights. Las Casas' philosophy was based on his objection to the *encomienda* system, by means of which Spanish colonizers acquired the right to exact taxes and service from a settlement of local inhabitants in return for providing them with protection and religious instruction. Las Casas believed that the *encomenderos*, acting as semi-feudal overlords, were responsible for the brutal exploitation and maltreatment of their Indian serfs. Proclaimed as the 'Protector of the Indians' in 1516, he urged the Crown, as the ultimate defender of justice and the Christian faith, to reclaim its authority over its newly conquered subjects in the

Americas and so liberate them from their rapacious oppressors. Las Casas was not the only person to question the legitimacy of the manner of conquest. The humanist scholar Francisco de Vitoria (c.1492–1546) pointed out in his *Relectio de Indis* (1539) that in their subjection of the indigenous peoples of the New World to their will, Spaniards had clearly used measures 'in excess of what is allowed by human and divine law'. A new colonial legal code was established in 1542 (the so-called 'New Laws of the Indies'), which considerably extended the ambit of the original Laws of Burgos (1512) to include the recommendation that Indian slavery and the *encomienda* system both be abolished within a generation. However, over the course of time the Laws became modified to the advantage of the settler community.[5]

Las Casas wrote his *Brevísima relación de la destrucción de las Indias* [*A Brief Account of the Destruction of the Indies*] in the same year that the New Laws were enacted, but he did not publish it until 1552, shortly after he had participated in a public debate (with the Aristotelian scholar Juan Ginés de Sepúlveda) on the ethics of imperial conquest, held at the University of Valladolid in 1550. According to Sepúlveda's *Democrates Alter* or *The Just Causes of the War against the Indians*, Spaniards were justified in subjecting inferior, barbaric peoples to their will in pursuit of their civilizing aims.[6] Las Casas fiercely challenged Sepúlveda's theory and stressed the natural right of the Indians to justice as equals of all men. Although there was no official outcome to the debate, other than allowing both sides to express their views, it spurred on Las Casas to publish his *Brief Account* and bring his on-going concerns to the attention of the future king, Philip II. In the work, he described with great passion the atrocities committed by Spaniards against innocent Indians from the vantage point of his own personal experience of being there, and prophesized that the actions of his countrymen would ultimately lead to their demise as a nation. 'I believe that because of these impious and ignominious deeds, so unjust, tyrannical and barbarously done in the Indies and against the Indians, God must certainly envelop Spain in his fury and anger',[7] he stated in his will. For Spaniards to treat the indigenous population like animals was against God's laws, the laws of nature, and those of Castile.

In the preface to his work, Las Casas described in the starkest terms the quest for material gain and disregard for humanity that he perceived had characterized the whole colonization enterprise:

> The reason why Spaniards have murdered on such a vast scale and killed anyone and everyone in their way is purely and simply greed. They have set out to line their pockets with gold and to amass private fortunes as quickly as possible so that they can then assume a status quite at odds with that unto which they were born. Their insatiable greed and overweening ambition knows no bounds; the land is fertile and rich, the inhabitants simple, forbearing and submissive. The Spaniards have shown not the slightest consideration for these people, treating them (and I speak from first-hand experience, having been there from the outset) not as brute animals ... so much as piles of dung in the middle of the road. They have had as little concern for their souls as for their bodies, all the millions that have perished having gone to their deaths with no knowledge of God and without the benefits of the Sacraments. One fact in all this is widely known and beyond dispute, for even the tyrannical murderers themselves acknowledge the truth of it: the indigenous peoples never did the Europeans any harm whatever; on the contrary, they believed them to have descended from the heavens, at least until they or their fellow-citizens had tasted, at the hands of these oppressors, a diet of robbery, murder, violence, and all other manner of trials and tribulations.[8]

Las Casas set out in his own words 'to make known to all Spain the true account and truthful understanding of what I have seen take place in this Indian Ocean'. He wrote, as he claimed, from the first-hand perspective of a real witness to events, and from this privileged position he sought to reveal the facts, including accounts of massacres of innocent people that were often concealed or falsified in the reports which royal officers in the Indies sent back to Spain. In reality, Las Casas did not set foot in those areas where the largest and most devastating conquests occurred – Central Mexico and Peru – but relied on second-hand, and arguably unreliable, evidence but which was readily accepted as trustworthy. In turning his personal testimony into written prose, he both used the language of the Gospels and drew associations between the Muslim destruction of Spain and the Christian destruction of America. The use of the word 'destruction' in the title of his account was an implicit reference to the earlier 'destruction' of Spain: the Arab invasion of 711. 'Spain was destroyed by Moors', he wrote in his work *Entre Remedies*, 'and it is rather to be believed that this was because of the sins of all the people and of the harm and evil they had done to their neigh-bours. And now we have heard many say, "Pray to God that he does not destroy Spain for the many evils which we have heard are committed in the Indies."'[9] Las Casas' prophetic claims of divine retribution, which played upon fears of an Ottoman advance in the Mediterranean, had powerful resonances for Spaniards. The conquistadors frequently compared their activities in the Indies to those of their forefathers in the Christian Reconquest of Spain. Upon arrival in the Americas, they often had masses said for their legendary hero in their struggle with the Moors: El Cid (Rodríguez Díaz de Vivar, c.1043–99). Las Casas pointed out that 'conquest', interpreted by Spaniards as 'victories', actually meant a barbarous attack and was 'iniquitous, tyrannical, contrary to natural, canon, and civil law'.[10] He reversed a common stereotype by equating the *conquerors*' behaviour to that of 'barbarians' – a term usually applied to those of non-Christian faith as well as to those who behaved like beasts or were culturally unsophisticated – instead of associating it with the *conquered*. In Las Casas' view, within the context of the Americas, it was the Europeans who were the 'savages' and the Indians who were the 'civilized'. As well as metaphorically challenging their faith, he thus completely trans-posed the relationship between 'them' and 'the other', dismantling Aristole's theory of natural slavery, based upon the innate inferior-ity of primitive civilizations, to prove that 'all the races of the world are men and the definition of all men, and of each of them, is only one and that is [he is of] reason'.[11] He described the indige-nous population as 'naturally so peace-loving, so humble and so docile',[12] using biblical references to Apostolic purity and natural innocence. The Spaniards, by contrast, are referred to in the way that medieval chroniclers used to speak of the Arab invaders of Spain, as 'ravening wolves ... or tigers and savage lions who have not eaten meat for days'.[13] Las Casas' rhetoric, which struck at the heart of Spaniards' Christian religious conscience and their perception of their own civility – the dual principles upon which mankind was classified as a social being – was designed to move his audience, essentially the king and the Council of Indies, and was no doubt exaggerated to impress upon his audience the magnitude of the event, such as when he wrote of 'more than twelve million souls, women and children among them' dying unwarranted deaths as a result of the 'despotic and diabolical behaviour of the Christians'.[14] Essentially, Las Casas did not doubt Spain's mission to the Indies or the spiritual purpose that under-pinned it, but he felt it should be pursued by peaceful means rather than via coercion. The *Brief Account* was written in protest at a juncture when it still seemed possible to reverse the damage wrought by Spanish colonization and restore the messianic purpose of the overseas mission in the Indies, although by the time the account was published, it was too late to turn the tide of history.

Originally intended to shock and persuade Spanish official-dom into taking radical corrective action to fully protect the rights of the indigenous population of the New World, Las Casas' *Brief Account* – withdrawn from publication in Spain in 1660 – was translated and used as propaganda by Spain's political and reli-gious enemies, and in that process the anti-Hispanic Black Legend came into being. His work was read by non-Spaniards in isolation, with no knowledge of the context in which it was written. We know that translations of the text, with lurid titles and illustra-tions, appeared in Dutch (1578), French (1579), English (1583) and German (1599), as well as other languages, and that as a result the reputation of Spaniards as people guilty of excesses and cruel-ties spread throughout the world. The Dutch translation of 1596 (*The Mirror of Spanish Tyranny in the West Indies*) was repub-lished in 1621 (the year in which the Truce with Spain ended) as *The Mirror of Spanish Tyranny in the Netherlands*. The 1656 English translation, by the puritan John Phillips, entitled *The Tears of the Indians: Being an Historical and True Account of the Cruel Massacres and Slaughters of Above Twenty Millions of Innocent People*, was addressed to Oliver Cromwell as Lord Protector of England (Figure 1). In the same year as its publication, Cromwell delivered a speech to Parliament in which he attacked Spaniards for their superstition, imperialism, cruelty, militarism and political intransigence, reasons that justified the English attack on Spanish colonies in the West Indies.[15] These examples provide an indica-tion of how the work was deliberately appropriated for purposes that the author never intended. Las Casas' text was frequently reproduced in conjunction with illustrations by the Flemish-born engraver and publisher Theodore de Bry (1528–98) which exposed Spanish atrocities, including horrific depictions of cannibalism. Thus a stereotypical image of barbarity and bigotry that underpinned Spanish colonialism became impressed upon the minds of future generations of Europeans and Americans, who associated Spain's treatment of pagan civilizations in the New World with its imperial policies in the Old. When the *Brief Account* was reprinted in later centuries, the implication was that the Spanish reputation for brutality had remained unchanged since the time of the American conquests. The various ways in which Las Casas has been interpreted by historians, as the voice of European Christian conscience, the liberator of the Indians-cum-father of Spanish-American independence, the outspoken critic of Spanish imperialism, the combatant friar, all account for the dialogue of interpretations that have informed the Black Legend through the centuries.[16]

Recent research has suggested that the powerful images by Theodore de Bry that accompanied Las Casas' text, depicting both the cruelty practised by New World colonizers as well as the barbarity of the Indian population itself, may have been simplistically or purposefully misinterpreted as the work of an anti-Spanish propagandist (Figures 2 and 3). De Bry's prints originally appeared in 1565 in the *History of the New World* (*Historia del Mondo Nuovo*) by the Italian traveller Girolamo Benzoni, in which he offered his own criticism of Spanish imperialism. A close reading of the preface to the 1594 Latin edition of Benzoni's work reveals how de Bry invited his readers not to condemn the Spaniards' behaviour in isolation but to recognize the destructive forces of greed, power and idolatry, as well as the susceptibility to sin, shared by the whole of humankind.

> Let us not be too quick to condemn the Spaniards and let us first seriously examine ourselves, in order to see if we are truly better than they are. I have, in effect, known among Spaniards many who were neither less pious nor less honest than those of any other nation. This I say without the slightest prejudice. Moreover, if Spaniards have often behaved in a cruel, greedy, and unjust fashion in the Indies, we must not impute such behaviour to their nation but to the license of soldiers, who, as we know, behave with equal cruelty whatever their

Figure 1 Frontispiece to Bartolomé de Las Casas' *Tears of the Indians*, London, 1656. © Trustees of the British Museum

nation of origin. Who ignores the numerous acts of violence perpe-
trated – and that are still committed now – by the French, German,
and Italian soldiers and others in almost all campaigns and wars?[17]

His perspective, therefore, can be interpreted as moral and philosophical rather than critical of Spanish colonization. Thus, in the
same way as *A Brief Account* has been misused by proponents of
the Black Legend for their own ends, so too have de Bry's images.

Where the development of the Black Legend in Europe is
concerned, information supplied by native Spanish Protestants
provided powerful ammunition for those northern European
countries that sought to highlight the Spanish Inquisition as
emblematic of a cruel and fanatical Spain. A work of seminal influence in impressing the Inquisition's 'brutish and beastly madness'
on the public imagination and exploiting its credulity was *Sanctae
Inquisitionis Hispanicae Artes* (*A Discovery of the Plaine*

Figure 2 Theodore de Bry, *Americae Pars Quarta*, 1594, Plate 16: Indians
take revenge on Spanish missionaries in the province of Cumana. © The
British Library Board. All rights reserved (C.115.h.2 (4))

Figure 3 Theodore de Bry, *Americae Pars Quarta*, 1594, Plate 22: Indians accused of sodomy eaten alive by dogs. © The British Library Board. All rights reserved (C.115.h.2 (4))

Declaration of Sundry Subtill Practices of the Holy Inquisition of Spaine) by the pseudonymous author Reginaldus Gonsalvius Montanus (1527–91), published in Latin in Heidelberg in 1567. Within a year it was reissued via Protestant printing presses in English, French, Dutch and German. The vivid style and imagination of Montanus turned the book into an immediate international success, and as it became incorporated into the mainstream of historical writing, so did the distortion and misrepresentation that it lent to its subject matter. It is generally assumed that the author's name is a pseudonym. *Montaña* (Montanus) in Spanish denotes somebody from the mountains of Asturias or Vizcaya, the ancestors of pure Old Christians, among whom the surname González (Gonsalvius) was commonplace. The writer was most likely to be Antonio del Corro, who was expelled from the

Hieronymite monastery of San Isidoro in Seville in 1557/58 along with other reform-minded monks (Dr Constantino de la Fuente and Dr Juan Egidio) as part of the Inquisition's ruthless campaign, orchestrated throughout Castile in the mid-sixteenth century, to destroy what it perceived to be the native roots of Protestantism on its shores. In 1557 del Corro fled to the Netherlands, where he converted to Lutheranism and composed his ferocious attack on the Spanish Inquisition, largely based on second-hand knowledge of its practices, passed by word of mouth.[18]

In his treatise, Montanus set out to argue that the Inquisition, initially constituted to persecute false or back-sliding *conversos*, was subsequently turned into a repressive instrument of secular control, intent on the destruction rather than the salvation and conversion of souls. 'The world may see', he wrote, 'that all the devices and policies of the Holy Inquisition tend to no other end, but after they have layd their cruell hands ... upon any person ... to destroy him both body and soul.'[19] He adopted the narrative device of guiding a would-be victim (the reader) through all stages of the inquisitorial process in order to emphasize its horrors in the most negative light possible, starting with their initial apprehension, the sequestration of their goods, their imprisonment, the hearing of evidence, including that of witnesses, the use of torture to extract a confession, through to the final judgements of inquisitors and the publication of the sentence. He placed heavy emphasis throughout on its coercive strategy, referring to the 'barbarous tyranny' of inquisitors who dealt with prisoners 'as men commonly use to intreat those men whom in derision of all humanity they terme dogges'.[20] On its judicial methods, he criticized the biased nature of defence counsels, the unreliability of witnesses' testimony and the untrustworthiness of interrogation techniques. He maintained that false allegations were frequently made of prisoners when sentences were pronounced 'which hee neyther spake nor thought in all his lifetime'.[21]

Montanus wrote in an extremely plausible style that led his readership to make assumptions about the Inquisition based on an exaggerated and sensationalized interpretation of its practices. He gave the impression that everyone who came under its jurisdiction was an innocent victim, that all of its officials were corrupt and that its practices contravened every single legal precedent. He made out that the Tribunal's sole efforts were directed at rooting out dubious theological propositions based on unsubstantiated evidence and that nobody stood a chance of disproving the case against them and of being reprieved. He, and fellow pamphleteers, clearly 'tampered with the facts' in order to present the most unfavourable and therefore most convincing case against the Holy Office. The tone of the narrative appealed directly to the political and religious sensitivities of his audience and helps to explain the work's wide dissemination. Montanus' description of the flagrant abuses of the Inquisition ran parallel to the condemnation of Spanish colonialism evidenced in Las Casas' work and further denigrated the character of Spain that had emerged over the course of the century. It suited Spain's Protestant enemies – England, France and the Netherlands in particular – to seize upon the evils of Spanish power and culture as a means of deflecting attention from their own problems of religious dissent and its repression, which arguably exposed them to similar accusations of inhumanity.[22]

The English translator of Montanus' work, Thomas Skinner, building upon the original commentary and adding his own touch of sensationalism, sought in his preface to the work of 1625 to instil fear in his readers as to what they could expect to witness if Roman Catholicism were to be again restored in England as it had been under Mary Tudor. He pointed as well to the fate of rebel subjects in the Spanish Netherlands:

> Surely, the dangerous practices and most horrible executions of the Spanish Inquisition declared in this boke, which now is brought with fire and sword into the low countries, the sodaine imprisonment of honest men, without process of lawe, the pitifull wandering in exile and poverty of personages sometimes rich and welthy, the wives hanging on their husbands shoulders, and the pore banished infants on the mothers brests, the monstrous racking of men without order of lawe, the villainous and shameless tormenting of naked women beyond all humanitie, their miserable deaths without pity or mercy, the most reproachfull triumphing of popish Sinagoge over Christians … the conquering of subiects as though they were enemies, the unsatiable spoyling of mennes goodes to fill the side paunches of ambitious idle shavelings, the slender quarrels picked against Kingdoms and Nations, and all this only to hoist up a pield polling priest [the Pope] above all power and authoritie that is on earth:

23

these things ought surely much more to move us to compassion. ... Wherefore (good Reader) having so evident markes of their wolvish and ravening natures, and so good notice of their bloody conspiracie, and so waying the very true cause of these troubles and warres that be in Christendome ... let us be stirred to pray for their deliver-ance.[23]

The *Acts and Monuments* (1563) of the Marian exile John Foxe (1517–87) also exercised a major influence on the English perception of Spanish Catholicism in the second half of the sixteenth century. Better known as *Book of Martyrs*, it was a popular, vividly written and widely circulated book – a Christian history with martyrdom as its central theme – that echoed the preoccupations of society upon the accession of Mary Tudor to the throne in 1553 and the fear that an English Inquisition would be revived to deal with dissenting Protestant 'heretics' in imitation of that operating in Spain. Foxe presented graphic accounts of acts of martyrdom in Christianity and linked the pagan persecutions of antiquity with those of more recent victims such as William Tyndale and Archbishop Cranmer. The 1570 edition of the book contained a section devoted to Spanish Protestant martyrs, includ-ing the cases of Constantino de la Fuente and Juan Egidio, drawn directly from the examples of martyrdom included in Montanus' work.[24] Foxe clearly framed his stories both to pay tribute to those who had sacrificed their lives for their beliefs and to denounce the persecution of heresy at home and abroad in such a way that served the efforts of the English Protestant Reformation, as well as promoting anti-Spanish, anti-Inquisition sentiment in northern Europe in general. He warned his readers that 'this dreadful engine of tyranny may at any time be introduced into a country where the Catholics have the ascendancy; and hence how careful ought we to be, who are not cursed with such an arbitrary court, to prevent its introduction'.[25] He gave a lurid description of 'the extreme dealing and cruel revenge of these Catholic Inquisitors of Spain', who, so he claimed, 'under the pretended visor of religion, do nothing but seek private gain and advantage, with crafty rifling and spoiling of other men's goods'.[26] Foxe's assertions about the Spanish Inquisition, which bear a striking resemblance to those of Montanus, approach the truth in broad terms, but by clever use of dramatization and hyperbole he contrived to paint a picture of its practices that was designed above all to instil fear and hatred of those responsible:

> The abuse of this inquisition is most execrable. If any word shall pass out of the mouth of any, which may be taken in evil part, yea, though no word be spoken, yet if they bear any grudge or evil will against the party, they command him to be taken, and put into a horrible prison, and then they find out crimes against him at their leisure, and in the meantime, no man living is so hardy as once to open his mouth for him. [...] Add moreover to the distresses and horrors of the prison, the injuries, threats, whippings and scourgings, irons, tortures and racks which they there endure. Sometimes they are also brought out, and shewed forth to the people in some high place as a symbol of rebuke and infamy. And thus they are detained there, some many years, and murdered by long torments, and whole days together are treated more cruelly out of all comparison, than if they were in the hangman's hands to be slain all at once.[27]

Montanus' work also had a major bearing on subsequent anti-Hispanic literature and thought, including the toleration debates of the seventeenth and eighteenth centuries in which political and religious thinkers attacked those nations who forced the consciences or inflicted punishment on others solely on the basis of their confessional identity. The Spanish Inquisition as drawn by the Dutch Remonstrant pastor Philip van Limborch (1633–1712) in his *History of the Inquisition* of 1692 was also heavily influenced by his reading of Montanus. His reproduction of carefully selected documentation on inquisitorial procedures was designed to demonstrate the iniquity of the tribunal via the words of its own officials and to hold up the Spanish Inquisition as the worst of the religious evils of Christian Europe that brought political and economic disaster to its nation and thus stood as a warning to all rulers who professed to deny liberties to dissenting subjects.[28]

The anti-Spanish propaganda that was generated via the printing presses from the mid-sixteenth century onwards, much of it based on myth and the proliferating genre of Hispanophobic literature circulating in northern Europe, was a significant factor in the development of the Dutch contribution to the Black Legend. The effectiveness of Dutch propaganda, translated into French, German and English, was due in large part to its emphatic condemnation of all that Spain stood for, set against the self-proclaimed untarnished reputation of its own nation. It incorporated four main themes: firstly, the diabolical nature of the Spanish Inquisition (influenced by the publication in Heidelberg of Montanus' work in 1567) and its likely introduction into the Spanish Netherlands; secondly, the private vices and crimes of Philip II; thirdly, the Spanish plans for universal empire; and fourthly, the inherent barbarity of Spaniards, as borne out in their treatment of the indigenous people of the Americas.[29] These indictments fuelled the intensive campaign on behalf of the Dutch rebels to denigrate Spain as an oppressive imperial power and ideological force and justified their action in waging war on it to achieve their independence as a nation.

William of Orange (1533–84), leader of the Dutch revolt against Spanish rule in the Netherlands from 1572 and self-styled 'patron of the fatherland and champion of freedom', addressed a speech (*Apology*) to the States General of the Netherlands in 1580, in which he claimed that the Dutch resistance to the violent methods unleashed by the Duke of Alba during his governorship (1568–73) to stamp out heresy was a legitimate reaction to the Spanish violation of their privileges and the attempt to reduce them to servitude. Written by a French Huguenot, it reflected the impact of Calvinist political thought and discourse upon the Netherlands and gave potent verbal ammunition to the rebels' cause. The *Apology* took the form of an exaggerated series of charges against Philip II (who had recently put a price on Orange's head), including what was to become the widely propagated myth that the king and the Inquisition were implicated in the death of his eldest son, Don Carlos, in 1568. The Spanish king is portrayed as a symbol of evil and oppression, a representation of the degeneracy and moral decadence of the Spanish people, intent on conquering a country whose lands formed part of the patrimony of the Holy Roman Empire, unto which they had given themselves voluntarily. According to Orange, Philip's cruelty and tyranny, in particular that exercised against innocent Indians, were but a foretaste of what would follow once he executed his plan to subdue the Netherlands to Spanish rule. Widely circulated through western Europe, the *Apology* made ample use of Las Casas' *Brief Account*, which first appeared in Dutch translation in 1578 and ran to thirty-three editions in the period up to 1648. By attributing the worst atrocities to the Spanish conquerors, it gave support to the notion that the Dutch population would suffer a similar fate under Spanish rule to that of the native Indian inhabitants of the New World:

> I have seene (my Lordes) their doings, I have hearde their wordes, I have bin a witnes of their advise, by which they adiudged all you to death, making no more account of you, than of beastes, if they had had the power to have murthered you, as they do in the Indies, where they have miserablie put to death, more than twentie millions of people, and have made desolate and waste, thirtie tymes as much lande in quantitie and greatnes, as the lowe countrie is, with such horrible excesses and ryottes, that all the barbarousnesses, cruelties, and tyrannies, whiche have ever bin committed, are but sport, in respect of that, which hath fallen out upon the poore Indians.[30]

The *Apology* also painted a sinister picture of the Inquisition as the usurper of political and civil liberties and the tyrannical force behind the policies of Philip II. It identified the threat posed by the establishment of the Inquisition in the Netherlands, operating under episcopal authority, as responsible for the Revolt and the 'reign of terror' that would follow. Orange warned in his *Apology* that 'all these their purposes, tending to no other ende, but to set upp the cruell Inquisition of Spaine, and to establishe the sayde Bishoppes, that they might serve, instead of Inquisitours, burners of mens bodies, and tyrauntes over their consciences'.[31] Furthermore, William of Orange's claim that 'the greatest parte of the Spanyardes, and specially those that counte themselves Noble men, are of the blood of Moores and Jews',[32] denigrated them to the infamous status of converts to Christianity and therefore of suspect faith – the worst form of opprobrium that could be applied to a ruling society that built its international reputation on the strength of its Catholic identity and mission. In essence, as an instrument of political propaganda, the *Apology*, which also found sympathetic readers in Elizabethan England and Huguenot France, provided a powerful stimulus for the growth of antipathy towards all that Spain stood for and validated views that then became enshrined in historical discourse for centuries.

Spain's own response to the Black Legend did not surface until the beginning of the twentieth century, when the Spanish right-wing journalist Julián Juderías (1877–1918) set out to prove in his book *La Leyenda Negra: Estudios acerca del concepto de España en el Extranjero* [*The Black Legend: Studies on foreign attitudes towards Spain*] (1914) that the 'black' image of Spain that had become integrated into the general history of European thought was distorted and based on myth and national prejudice built up over the centuries. He identified most of the writers who contributed to the Black Legend as staunch, even fanatical Protestants. Their hatred of Spain, so he claimed, was based primarily on envy of its imperial strength and prejudice with regard to its Catholic status. Hence they drew an exaggerated picture of Spaniards' treatment of heretics by the Inquisition and their use of force to Christianize pagan peoples in the New World. These prejudices, according to Juderías, sustained the legend of 'an inquisitorial, ignorant, fanatical Spain, incapable of taking its place among civilized peoples either now or in the past, predisposed always to violent repression and an enemy of progress and innovation ... born out of the Reformation, it has not ceased to be used against us since'.[33]

Juderías agreed that Spain had once been an intolerant nation, but argued that so too had been other nations in the course of their history. A major error of Black Legend literature, in his view, had been to identify Spain as exclusively responsible and to extend the charge into later periods, when it became irrelevant. As a result, a serious misrepresentation of Spain's historical role had occurred. Juderías acknowledged that, to some extent, Spaniards helped to foster the legend by virtue of the lack of a strong native historiographical tradition via which to refute it. Hence it had lived on uncontested into modern times:

> Although it is sad to have to admit it, we are principally to blame for the cultivation of the Black Legend, for two principal reasons: firstly, because we have not studied our own history with the same interest and detail as foreigners have their own history and, lacking this foundation, we have informed ourselves from books written by foreigners and inspired, in part, by contempt for our nation; secondly, because we have always fostered misinformation and harsh criticism.[34]

Juderías's work marked the beginning of the rehabilitation of Spain from Black Legend mythology and was followed by other studies, including Rómulo de Carbia's *Historia de la leyenda negra hispano-americana* [*History of the Hispano-American Black Legend*], published in 1943, which set out to establish the true historical facts on the use of cruelty in the conquest of the Americas. From his research into the testimony of other eyewitnesses to events, Carbia concluded that the crimes and abuses attributed to colonizers were more sporadic than regular, demonstrating that Las Casas' *Brief Account* was excessive in tone, as was the anti-Hispanic historical discourse that it generated.[35]

Invented as a tool of Protestant propaganda in the sixteenth century, the Black Legend characterized Spain as a bastion of intolerance, ignorance and bigotry. It was subsequently adopted by generations of historians up to the twentieth century to explain the gap that opened up between the backwardness and poverty of Spain and the advancement of the prospering nations of northern Europe, themes that underpinned the whole decline debate. A counterpart White Legend was promoted as a reaction to these accusations by those who sought to defend Spain's orthodox tradition, upheld as the essence of its identity and the foundation of its imperial greatness.[36] From the dialectic of the two legends, the notion of 'Two Spains' entered into the collective consciousness and became part of the ideological and political construct of modern Spain.

Notes

1 Sverker Arnoldsson, *La Leyenda Negra. Estudios sobre sus orígenes* (Gotheburg, 1960), pp. 91–9. All translations from Spanish sources by the author.

2 Cited by K.W. Swart, 'The Black Legend during the Eighty Years War', in J.S. Bromley and E.H. Kossman (eds), *Britain and the Netherlands*, Vol. 5 (The Hague, 1975), p. 36.

3 Barbara Fuchs, 'The Spanish Race', in Margaret R. Greer et al. (eds), *Rereading the Black Legend* (Chicago, IL, 2007), p. 96.

4 Charles Gibson (ed.), *The Black Legend. Anti-Spanish Attitudes in the Old World and the New* (New York, 1971) reproduces extracts from the discourse.

5 A.R. Pagden, Introduction to Bartolomé de Las Casas, *A Short Account of the Destruction of the Indies*, trans. N. Griffin (Harmondsworth, 1992), pp. xviii–xxx.

6 Antony Pagden, Introduction to *A Short* Account, pp. xxvii–xxx.

7 Cited by Pagden, Introduction to *A Short Account*, p. xxxviii.

8 Las Casas, *A Short Account*, preface, p. 13.

9 Cited by Pagden, Introduction to *A Short Account*, p. xxxviii.
10 Las Casas, *A Short Account*, prologue, p. 6.
11 Cited by Antony Pagden, *The Fall of Natural Man: The American Indian and the Origins of Comparative Ethnology* (Cambridge, 1992), p. 140.
12 Las Casas, *A Short Account*, prologue, p. 6.
13 Ibid., preface, p. 11.
14 Ibid., p. 12.
15 Gibson, *The Black Legend*, pp. 54–62.
16 Ibid., pp. 13–14; Pagden, Introduction to *A Short Account*, pp. xiii–xiv.
17 P. Gravatt, 'Rereading Theodore de Bry's Black Legend', in Margaret R. Greer et al. (eds), *Rereading the Black Legend* (Chicago, IL, 2007), p. 241.
18 B.A. Vermaseren, 'Who Was Reginaldus Gonslavius Montanus?', *Bibliotheque d'Humanisme et Renaissance*, 43 (1985), 47–77; Gordon A. Kinder, 'Spain's Little-known "Noble Army of Martyrs" and the Black Legend', in L.K. Twomey (ed.), *Faith and Fanaticism in Early Modern Spain* (Aldershot, 1987), pp. 61–83.
19 Gonsalvius Reginaldus Montanus, *A Discovery and Plaine Declaration of sundry subtill practices of the Holy Inquisition of Spaine*, translated by Thomas Skinner (London, 1625), chap. v, p. 41.
20 Ibid., chap. x, p. 71.
21 Ibid., chap xii, p. 102.
22 Edward Peters, *Inquisition* (Berkeley and Los Angeles, CA, 1989), pp. 133–4.
23 Montanus, *Holy Inquisition of Spaine*, Translator to the Reader, pp. A3–B3, cited by Peters, *Inquisition*, pp. 139–40.
24 William S. Maltby, *The Black Legend in England. The Development of Anti-Spanish Sentiment, 1558–1660* (Durham, NC, 1971), pp. 33–43.
25 John Foxe, *Book of Martyrs* (Hartford, CT, 1845), Book V, p. 104.
26 Foxe, *Book of Martyrs* (London, 1888 edition), Book IX, p. 884.
27 Ibid., p. 174.
28 Peters, *Inquisition*, pp. 166–70; Francisco Bethencourt, *The Inquisition. A Global History, 1478–1834* (Cambridge, 2009), pp. 5–7.
29 Swart, 'The Black Legend during the Eighty Years War', p. 38.
30 H. Wansink (ed.), *The Apologie of Prince William of Orange against the Proclamation of the King of Spaine* (Leiden, 1969), pp. 58–9.
31 *Apologie*, p. 99.
32 Ibid., p. 137.
33 Julián Juderías, *La Leyenda Negra*, p. 14. Part of Juderías' work is available in English translation in Jon Cowans (ed.), *Modern Spain. A Documentary History* (Philadelphia, PA, 2003), pp. 111–14.
34 Julián Juderías, *La Leyenda Negra*, p. 17.
35 Rómulo D. Carbia, *La leyenda negra hispano-americana* (Madrid, 2004), pp. 57–68.
36 Note that Benjamin Keen in 'The Black Legend Revisited: Assumptions and Realities', *The American Historical Review*, 49:4 (1969), 703–19, refers to a different understanding of the White Legend as 'a counter legend of Spanish altruism and benevolence towards the Indians', 719.

2

The seventeenth century: *arbitrisimo* and decline

I am sir, an *arbitrista* and at different times I have provided His Majesty with every sort of expedient, each designed to be of benefit to him and his kingdom. (Miguel de Cervantes, *Exemplary Stories: The Dogs' Coloquy* (1613), trans. C.A. Jones [Harmondsworth, 1984], p. 249)

The opening decades of the seventeenth century witnessed the publication of an unprecedented volume of polemical literature in Spain written by contemporary observers in response to the acute economic crisis engulfing its kingdoms. A hundred and sixty-five tracts were published between the beginning of the reign of Philip III in 1598 and the end of that of Philip IV in 1665, penned by a heterogeneous group of commentators drawn from diverse professions, collectively known as *arbitristas* or 'projectors'. They put forward a range of expedients (*arbitrios*) for restoring Spanish power to its former glory that reflected their varied experiences and outlooks on Spain's past and present. Such was their collective concern at their nation's plight that they felt duty bound to advise the monarch on ways and means to support it and save it from collapse. Some of their proposals were examined within government circles and influenced policy decisions. The *arbitristas* can be regarded as the first generation of historians to address the phenomenon of Spain's decline, and from the standpoint of direct witnesses to events.

Although criticized by their contemporaries for the sweeping, exaggerated nature of some of their judgements – they were satirized as meddlers (*barbitristas*) in the writing of Quevedo and as dreamers by Cervantes in *Don Quixote* and *The Exemplary Novels* – *arbitrista* discourse has been favourably re-assessed by modern scholars. Some of the most respected contributors to the debate included the lawyer Martín González de Cellorigo; the priest and university professor Sancho de Moncada; the royal doctor Cristóbal Pérez de Herrera; members of the Council of Castile; the royal chaplain and secretary Pedro Fernández de Navarrete; and the diplomat Diego Saavedra Fajardo. The *arbitristas'* agenda included observations on the inflated perception of wealth derived from Spain's discovery of the New World alongside criticisms of the cost of imperial defence, foreign influence in commercial and economic life, the lack of investment in agriculture, the restrictions placed on industry, the ever-growing burden of taxation, the false aristocratic values that pervaded society, as well as elitist attitudes towards labour and race. Political theorists and economists, as well as members of the Cortes (parliament), also joined in what was, given the age and climate, a remarkably open forum of public debate. When viewed collectively, their writings provide subsequent generations of historians with a unique insight into how Spaniards perceived their nation's decline and set the framework for the whole historiographical debate that was to follow.[1]

The various ways in which contemporary observers sought to explain the condition of their nation are fundamental, for these enable us to appreciate their evaluation of unfolding events, to enter what has been described as 'a laboratory of decline' and gauge its temperature. In assessing the reasons for their country's downfall, many looked back in their history to 'good times', most notably the age of Ferdinand and Isabella, when, according to González de Cellorigo, 'our Spain in all things reached its highest degree of perfection and greatness',[2] before falling into its current state of misery. The *arbitristas* are most commonly associated with formulating economic solutions to Spain's difficulties, but they also looked to God for spiritual guidance in examining their human actions and moral behaviour, as well as seeking fatalistic explanations in the recurrent cycle of nature.

In was logical that, given the profound religious identity of Spanish society in which the ordering of events reflected God's purpose, observers should search their souls for answers. This was a nation that had, in their eyes, been raised to greatness by the grace of God for its efforts to extirpate heresy and spread the faith among heathen peoples. Now, so it appeared, the tables were turned and divine providence was deemed to be instrumental in their downfall. This sense of retribution was shared by the *arbitristas*. 'O judgement of God, by what ways does Our Lord choose to punish our wretched Spain!'[3] pronounced Sancho de Moncada in 1619. Cast aside by God, they needed to win back his favour by strengthening their faith, respecting basic Christian values and curbing vices and excesses. A direct equation was drawn between morality and national well-being. In part, decline thus came to be perceived in terms of a decay in patterns of moral behaviour, emanating from the monarch and royal court, resulting from the transition of society from an age of simplicity and virtue to one of greed and corruption that had followed on from the discovery of the New World.[4]

Contemporaries also sought natural deterministic explanations for their predicament, linked to the movement of the planets and their effect on the universe. The idea of the rise and decline of states as forming part of a natural process that ran parallel to the growth and subsequent decay of all living matter was widely accepted in European thought. According to this logic, therefore, Spain's fall from political hegemony was an inevitable consequence of its period of supremacy, in imitation of the fate that befell the Roman Empire. Their very use of the word decline (*declinación*) can be seen to derive from this association. In practice, the historical paradigm was somewhat removed from *arbitristas*' general economic reflections on the reasons for Spain's decline, but the Roman parallel no doubt served psychologically to help justify their arguments. The first chapter of González de Cellorigo's treatise addressed the issue of 'how our Spain, however fertile and abundant it may be, is subject to the decline to which all republics are prone'. Jerónimo de Ceballos, a lawyer and local councillor from Toledo, in his treatise of 1623 observed a 'similarity between the government of a polity and the human body, which also suffers from excess or natural causes; and the same thing happens to the republic, which goes into decline either by bad government ... or by natural causes which proceed from time itself ... for everything which has a beginning must decline towards its end, just like the rising and the setting sun'.[5] Although a belief in fatalism and astrological determinism, linked to the transitory cycle of life, was not consistent with Christian belief, optimism and faith in deliverance, combined with a deep sense of patriotism, was never far removed from an acceptance of the preordained. González de Cellorigo observed that 'the illness of our republic is not so malign as to remove all hope of a remedy, if it is properly applied'.[6] Fernández de Navarrete wrote that 'the illness is very serious ... but not incurable'.[7] Hence the numerous antidotes that poured from the pens of the *arbitristas* as they took on the guise of doctors curing a sick patient, advising on the appropriate action to take to ensure a full recovery.

The *arbitristas* called for a programme of national regeneration and renewal to reverse Spain's fortunes. Its principal aims were to restore good government, revive the economy, maximize human potential and reform the moral fibre of society, including a curb on ostentatious and excessive indulgence in material pleasures, as well as the eradication of corruption in all walks of life. In the face of *declinación*, therefore, the key counter words (echoed in the titles of the various treatises themselves) were *restauración, reformación, remedio, reparo, conservación* and *desempeño* – restoration, reform, remedy, repair, preservation and redemption of debts. *Arbitrista* literature thus pointed towards Spain moving out of its decline and into a new, 'restorative' phase of its history. This implied actively seeking solutions to revive Spain's ailing condition, rather than passively accepting the inevitability of defeat. In their discourses, the *arbitrista* School relied heavily on the use of rhetoric and metaphor, drawn from classical writers such as Seneca, Aristotle and Pliny, as well as theological and philosophical points of reference, to persuade the reader (usually the king and senior ministers) that the particular remedies being proposed held the key to solving the nation's problems, the extent of which were frequently exaggerated for dramatic effect. Language, therefore, was a powerful tool of political influence and negotiation for contemporary writers seeking to capture public attention.[8]

In the context of the debate that followed, there emerged two fundamental and potentially conflicting routes which Spain could take to restore its greatness and which are echoed in subsequent literature: either to look to the past for inspiration or to move forward and seek new ways of dealing with Spain's problems. Here were the seeds of the 'Two Spains' phenomenon – the struggle between traditionalism, on the one hand, and liberalism, on the other – that had begun to emerge within Black Legend literature and was to shape its historical trajectory and discourse for generations to come. There has been a tendency among historians to attribute Spain's 'failure' as a nation to its adherence to the traditional order. However, it is important to emphasize that the eventual dominance of conservatism was born out of a vigorous ideological and political conflict with proponents of a reformist agenda over the future direction of their country.[9] In the short term, the idealism of the *arbitristas* was to clash with the interests of the political elite and the immediate prioritization of the needs of war over those of reform.

In their efforts to rationalize Spain's predicament, the *arbitristas* were heavily but not exclusively inclined towards the mercantilist economic theories that circulated widely throughout Europe in the sixteenth and seventeenth centuries. Spanish mercantilism grew out of the doctrines upheld by a school of theologians and jurists based at the University of Salamanca in the sixteenth century, led by Francisco de Vitoria (c.1492–1546), Domingo de Soto (1494–1560), Martín de Azpilcueta (1491–1586) and Luis de Molina (1535–1600), who applied the teachings of Thomas Aquinas (1224–75) to the contemporary political, ethical and economic order and became known as 'The School of Salamanca'. Mercantilist thinking was embedded in much *arbitrista* literature as a set of criteria that aimed to strengthen Spain's economic prosperity by protecting its monetary assets, regarded as its principal source of wealth, and reducing the outflow of precious metals.[10] The broader tenets of Spanish mercantilism were to discourage the export of raw materials and the import of manufactured goods by means of protectionist legislation and to spare no effort to encourage Spanish agriculture and industry, supported by a healthy active population.

One of the works that most influenced *arbitrista* thought was Giovanni Botero's *Reason of State* (1589), a book widely disseminated in Spain at the end of the sixteenth century, whose 'science of government', broadly based on mercantilist principles, could be

35

applied to cure the ills of state and society. Botero challenged the Machiavellian tradition of political theory by elaborating a Christian method for the preservation and development of powerful states. *Reason of State* was soon to become the quintessential guide for Christian government in Counter-Reformation Europe.[11] One of the essential virtues he identified in a successful ruler was prudence: a combination of moral strength and political aptitude, talents that would ensure he maintained his all-important reputation, and so his princely power. Botero used a number of measures to indicate the 'health' of nations. These included the fate of empires, demographics, the productivity of agriculture and industry and the flow of money. He warned against the negative repercussions of empire building, 'for greatness leads to self-confidence, confidence to negligence and negligence to contempt and loss of prestige and authority. Power breeds wealth, which is the parent of pleasure as pleasure is of all the vices; and this is why empires fall away from the height of their prosperity, for valour diminishes with increase of power and virtue with accretion of wealth.'[12] He saw the key to a nation's prosperity lying in its human resources: 'The true strength of a ruler ... consists in his people; for upon them depend all of his other resources. The ruler who has plenty of men will have plenty of everything which the ingenuity and industry of man can provide.'[13] On the economy he advised that 'A prince ... should encourage and promote agriculture ... and must keep alive and flourishing whatever serves to make his country fertile and highly productive of all that it can provide' and that 'a ruler must ensure that money does not leave his country unless this is quite essential ... for once money is sent out of the country it is lost and its potentialities are lost too'.[14] Contemporaries could not fail to be aware that the areas Botero highlighted as fundamental to national wealth and power, when applied to Castile, presented a clear contrast with its current fortunes.[15] His thesis was to provide an important framework for the seventeenth-century debate that followed.

Martín González de Cellorigo (15??-16??) was a pioneering member of the *arbitrista* generation of writers with a far-reaching modern economic vision that derived from the ideas of the Salamanca School. He worked as a lawyer at the *Real Chancillería* (Royal judicial tribunal) in Valladolid, where he witnessed first-hand the devastating effects of plague, hunger, disease and death that ripped through the region between 1599 and 1601. This experience undoubtedly influenced the writing of his treatise, *Memorial de la política necesaria y útil restauración de la república de España* [*The Restoration of the Spanish Republic*], published in 1600.[16] In this work, informed by his knowledge of canon and civil law, as well as classical antecedents, he proposed a fundamental review of state finances, the market economy and the taxation system in order to restore the monarchy to good health and solvency. Of major concern to him was the decline in the population that had formerly made Spain rich and powerful, as well as the misconceived idea of wealth, seen to originate from its stock of precious metals rather than the nation's productive capacity:

> And the whole trouble stems from the fact that we have scorned society's natural laws that require us to work for a living and presume that wealth derives from gold and silver, when in fact it is acquired through natural and human industry and that is why our republic has declined so greatly from its former state. [...] So one can indeed say that the wealth that should have enriched us has made us poor and as a result of its misuse merchants do not trade, farmers do not work the land, and there are many needy people who suffer from ill health.[17]

He felt a deep sympathy for the plight of the peasantry, attributing their rural distress to the heavy rental burden, 'for having paid the tithes owed to God, they pay an even greater amount to the owner of the land; and then follows innumerable obligations, impositions, payment of debts and dues, quite apart from the various state taxes to which they are subjected'.[18] From his position at the base of the social pyramid, the peasant farmer supported those at the top, leaving him precious little surplus for his own needs. Was it surprising, therefore, that many left the land, when even begging and petty crime provided a more secure living? His (no doubt exaggerated) estimate was that the proportion of workers to non-workers was one to thirty.

However, he firmly believed that the nation could recover from its setbacks by proper investment in agriculture, industry and enterprise as legitimate means of economic growth within the context of Christian statecraft rather than living from credit and indulging in material consumption that contradicted its precepts.

He perceived Spain to be a potentially wealthy nation, but one whose wealth was being 'dissipated on thin air – on papers, contracts, *censos* (annuities on loans), and letters of exchange, on cash and silver, and gold – instead of being expended on goods that yield profits and attract riches from outside to augment the riches within. And thus there is no money, gold, or silver in Spain because there is so much; and it is not rich, because of all its riches.'[19] He stressed the need to reconsider the value of work over leisure and reduce the quantity of 'professional' idlers and parasites in Spain. He warned that Spaniards' rejection of manual labour (associated with those of Jewish and *converso* blood) in favour of the preservation of honour and appearances (associated with the nobility and membership of the prestigious military orders[20]) was having detrimental consequences:

> What has so distracted our people from carrying out a legitimate occupation ... has been the emphasis placed on honour and the prestige attached to idleness. Those who engage in agriculture, business, commerce and any sort of manufacture are held in little esteem. And even the military orders do not admit anyone of mercantile stock. Thus it seems that we have become a republic of enchanted men living outside the natural order of things.[21]

The polarization of society that ensued severely impeded the development of a productive workforce:

> Our republic has come to be an extreme contrast of rich and poor, and there is no means of adjusting one to another. Our condition is one in which we have rich who loll at ease, or poor who beg, and we lack people of the middling sort, whom neither wealth nor poverty prevent from pursuing the rightful kind of business enjoined by natural law ... As a result, those who want to cannot, and those who can, do not want to ... and many projects necessary for the good of the republic remain undone.[22]

According to González de Cellorigo, Spain must rouse itself to become a nation dedicated to manufacturing and commerce and abandon its adherence to an elitist philosophy of 'he who does not live from a rental income cannot be considered to be a nobleman'.[23] Merchants, traders and farmers, rather than being regarded as inferiors, should be valued for their usefulness to society. The deployment of human industry and endeavour in pursuit of the economic and moral good of the nation was, for González de Cellorigo, the key to Spain's recovery. The perceptiveness of his testimony was matched by few subsequent commentators.

Toledo – the principal mercantile and industrial city of the southern Meseta for much of the sixteenth century – experienced an acute downturn in its economic and demographic fortunes during the period 1590–1620/30, symptomatic of that being felt throughout Castile, prompting the writing of numerous tracts by a 'Toledan School' of *arbitrista* writers. Sancho de Moncada (1578/79?–1635?), a priest and professor of theology at the University of Toledo, can be regarded as the most representative member of this School to espouse a mercantilist approach to solving Spain's economic ills. Moncada came from a family of local doctors and merchants and was most probably of Jewish descent. He may have taken up the clerical vocation, along with other relatives, to ensure a living in turbulent times, a phenomenon he alluded to in his treatise. In accordance with the close relationship that existed between church and state at this time, his professional background and educative role in society equipped him to act in an advisory capacity on matters pertaining to the good of the monarchy. Given the intellectual and cultural environment in which he moved, Moncada would have encountered a variety of approaches – theological, philosophical, political and economic – to the issues confronting society. His theoretical approach shares much in common with that of Luis de Ortiz, regarded as the pioneer of Spanish mercantilism, whose *Memorial al Rey para que no salgan dineros de Espana* (*Brief to the King on preventing monies leaving Spain*) of 1558, addressed to Philip II, Moncada would no doubt have known.

In his treatise *Restauración Política de España* [*The Political Restoration of Spain*], published in 1619, Moncada proposed a series of eight measures or *discursos*, each designed to increase Spain's prosperity. At the heart of his thinking lay the need to implement a complete ban on the entry of foreign merchants and merchandise. In his opinion, 'Spain is impoverished because French, Flemish, Genoese and Venetian merchants have cornered all the commercial contracts, resulting in the decline of mercantile cities such as Toledo, Burgos, Medina and Seville.'[24] He calculated that 80 per cent of trade with Spain and 90 per cent of trade with the Indies was in the hands of foreigners who were responsible for 'bleeding' Spain at the rate of 20 million ducats per year and fostering idleness – the father of all vices – among local merchants: 'So the Indies is theirs and Your Majesty's share of the fleet is all assigned to them.'[25] The exclusion of foreign traders, some of whom were associated with Protestant countries, would provide the opportunity to reinvigorate the Spanish manufacturing industry and revive Spain's economic fortunes. 'The whole remedy lies in Spain producing its own goods,'[26] he insisted. Moncada recognized that the protectionist mercantile policy he advocated, given the abundance of precious metals in the economy, would present some technical and material challenges, but Spain had to break with the inertia that had condemned it to serve as the slave of its European commercial partners. It had to earn its own living, relying on its own natural resources, in order to escape the cycle of poverty, death and emigration that had severely weakened it as a nation. 'Foreigners defraud us of large sums of money', he observed, 'permanently removing silver and goods, without returning anything to the economy.'[27] In essence, he called for a radical 'nationalization' of the economy, the impact of which would extend beyond the confines of Toledo to include the different component parts of the Empire, which he saw working best in a dynamic, complementary fashion.

Alongside the problem of foreign intervention in economic life, Moncada also drew attention to the reduction in size of the active labour force, which he attributed principally to plague, disease and a reluctance to marry and have children. From local baptismal records for the period 1617–18, he calculated that there had been a 50 per cent decline in marriage, as well as a failure to procreate. 'People no longer get married because they have no money to buy food and set up house together,'[28] he observed. He proposed a reform of the tax system, to include contributions from foreign merchants to the payment of the *alcabala* (sales tax) and the total abolition of the *millones* (tax on basic food items), as well as a reduction in royal dependency on foreign loans. In addition, he called for measures to improve the fertility and productivity of the land, as well the removal from the royal court of those dignitaries and officials who were there for reasons of status rather than necessity, as well as idle folk. He also recommended stricter controls on the number (and quality) of those seeking entry into the priesthood and religious orders, since the kingdom could not support so many who did not contribute to the economy: 'Those that enter the Church do not leave it and pay no taxes',[29] he wrote, and 'although their role is considered to be important, the kingdom cannot sustain as many, since the majority of those who used to provide alms for others, now seek charity for themselves'.[30] Finally, he advocated the expulsion of gypsies – considered to be nothing but layabouts and petty thieves – from Spain. These measures, so he argued, would help to restore the social and fiscal imbalance, providing more people to engage actively and productively in labour, commerce and agriculture, thus reducing the tax burden of the masses and raising royal revenues. Moncada proposed pragmatic solutions, spelled out in no-nonsense terms and articulated with a sense of urgency, to revive the economy.

Cristóbal Pérez de Herrera (1558–1620) differed from other *arbitristas* in so far as his proposals were essentially aimed at the welfare of society but, if carried forward, promised positive economic outcomes. Herrera derived from a family of Jewish converts to Chrisitianty (*conversos*) and had worked as a physician on the Spanish galleys as well as at the royal court, where he gained entrance to political circles via his friendship with the President of the Council of Castile, Rodrigo Vázquez de Arce, and began to write political treatises that reflected his concerns about socio-economic matters. In his *Discurso del amparo de los legítimos pobres* [*Discourse on the protection of the poor*] of 1598, dedicated to Philip III, he addressed the need to eradicate poverty and mendicancy from society, which he regarded as a fundamental economic necessity to increase prosperity, over and above a moral one to dispense Chrisitian charity and rescue the wayward:

> The first and greatest problem is that we seem to have in these kingdoms too many people who are false beggars, mingled with others who are genuine ones. [...] The second is the idle nature of their lives ... lending itself to sin and prostitution. [...] The third is that these people are so greedy that although they spend next to nothing, they accumulate a lot of money. [...] The fourth is, without fear of God, they are drawn into this low life style and instead of working,

they make out they have wounds . . . and pretend to be deaf and blind when they are not. [. . .] The fifth problem is, those that pretend to be poor get involved in thefts . . . and sow damage.[31]

Inspired by his reading of other writers on the subject of poverty, notably Juan Luis Vives [*De subventione pauperum*] (1526) and Miguel de Girginta [*Tractado de remedio de pobres*] (1579), he proposed the establishment of a number of poor houses or shelters (*albergues*) in fifty of the heaviest populated towns in Spain where the poor would come to be registered and their needs be assessed. The purpose was to distinguish between the true and false destitute. The genuine poor would be given shelter and an official permit to beg, while wayward and indolent male vagabonds who chose begging as an alternative to an honest living would be forced to work in areas most useful to the economy, learning new trades as necessary, or serve on the galleys. Female delinquents who practised prostitution would be identified and forced to work in a penitentiary. The most able poor youths would be offered university scholarships to broaden their intellectual horizons. The success of his project was dependent upon work being available for those who chose to take it up and the deployment of secular officials to enforce the regulations. Herrera's objective was to redeem the value of labour and therefore stimulate economic growth: to rescue those condemned by choice or default to a life of vagrancy, not only as a means of counteracting poverty, but in order to mobilize the active workforce for the benefit of the whole nation-state. Herrera's discourse responded to the need to rid society of deprivation and to convert the destitute into useful citizens. He believed that penury was as much a product of idleness as of prevailing economic conditions. The poor, 'by taking up occupations and roles that are necessary for the life of the nation . . . can be honourable, virtuous individuals who serve God and the republic'.[32] For Herrera, public welfare was essential to the conservation and expansion of the monarchy and he saw young people as being central contributors to this enterprise. He was optimistic about the prospects:

> Since we have metals and materials for everything, and there will be enough to occupy part of those who otherwise would be well on their way to becoming vagabonds and incorrigibles [. . .] and your

Majesty will no longer have occasion to employ for these purposes people of different nations, subjects of other kings and republics ... brought over at much expense and lacking our faith and loyalty.[33]

In this sense his theory coincided with the mercantilist projects of fellow *arbitristas* exhorting the employment of Spain's native resources to generate productivity rather than relying on foreign intervention. Furthermore, his programme opened up the possibility of class mobility and social advancement through the promotion of education and training to produce a skilled workforce. But the monarchy of Philip III was not ready for such practical yet far-reaching solutions to poverty and poor relief, and Herrera's proposals were shelved.[34]

In June 1618, given the acute crisis that his government faced on numerous fronts and the increasing level of concern being voiced by the Castilian Cortes at the monarchy's mounting debts alongside its lavish expenditure, Philip III, via his favourite, the Duke of Lerma, was moved to instruct the President of the Council of Castile to prepare a reform programme for the kingdom. It was written by one of Castile's councillors, Don Diego de Corral y Arrellano, and published just over six months later on 1 February 1619.[35] It was a measure of the gravity of the problems afflicting the kingdom that Castile's highest tribunal produced an agenda for the state's recovery. According to the Council of Castile's report entitled *Consulta sobre el remedio universal de los daños del Reino y reparo de ellos* [*Measures to stem the decline and promote the recovery of the kingdom*], the causes of decline were essentially the product of short-sighted government policy and gross mismanagement of its resources. In this sense the 1619 *Consulta* represented a direct attack on Philip III's monarchy, which was characterized by its irresponsibility in the distribution of patronage and office and crippling levels of taxation, coupled with mounting government debt.

Of primary concern to the Council was Castile's demographic downturn. The *Consulta* highlighted the main cause of depopulation as being the excessive burden of taxation experienced by agricultural workers in certain regions, resulting in families migrating to other (less fertile) regions, not subject to such pressures: 'Demographic decline has come about as a result of the heavy financial demands imposed upon Your Majesty's subjects.

Unable to bear such a burden and to escape dying of hunger, they have been forced to leave their wives, children and homes and go to seek a better life in other areas where they hope to survive.'[36] Councillors called for a reduction in the fiscal burdens carried by the peasantry and their redirection to other sectors of society. The report also placed emphasis on the disparity between the weight of royal generosity and conspicuous consumption set against a back-drop of national hardship. Councillors advised the Crown to urgently release funds by reviewing the liberal granting of pensions and rewards paid for directly from the royal exchequer. 'Although it is true that princes ennoble themselves by their generosity, this has to be within limits and subject to due temper-ance, since this virtue can give way to contrary vices',[37] they observed. The Council criticized the growth of the court, which had been achieved at the expense of repopulating other areas of the kingdom. It recommended that courtiers return to their aban-doned regions and regenerate them: 'The number of people that there are at court is excessive and it would be advisable to remove some of them and send them back to their places of origin.'[38] The tribunal advised that austerity laws should be introduced to curb excessive expenditure on luxury imports linked to vice, sin and corruption, with the monarch himself taking the lead: 'It would befit Your Majesty to apply the same degree of moderation in dress in the royal household, so that others might moderate and correct their habits by way of imitation.'[39] Finally, councillors of Castile proposed that a limit should be set on the foundation of new religious houses, since they encouraged idleness in place of productivity and false rather than true vocations, passing the economic burden on to secular society: 'Be cautious in giving licences for the foundation of religious houses, since many people are admitted to them who are more intent on escaping from want into a life of sweet leisure rather than being motivated by sense of true vocation.'[40] The *Consulta* set an agenda for reform with a practical focus and placed the onus firmly on the king to remedy the problems it outlined. Although the report, at best, met with a lukewarm response from Philip III and his government, it was considered sufficiently important to be reproduced in summary form for the attention of the new king, Philip IV, at the beginning of his reign three years later.

Pedro Fernández de Navarrete (1580–1632?), a canon of the cathedral church of Santiago and chaplain to the brother of Philip IV, was commissioned to write an extended commentary or gloss on the 1619 *Consulta*, published in 1626 as *Conservación de Monarquías* [*Conservation of Monarchies*], and dedicated to the President of the Council of Castile. Although he essentially dealt with issues similar to those covered by the *Consulta*, his emphasis varied, in keeping with his clerical status. Navarrete saw the major political, social and economic problems being faced by Spain as different manifestations of a central one: the abandonment of moral values and traditions that had underpinned its greatness as a nation.

While he accepted the ideological necessity of Spain's Catholic mission, he regretted its secular outcomes. The riches of empire, against which Spain set such great store, inspired vanity, over-indulgence and sloth, values that had damaging repercussions on society, as witnessed in the quest for aristocratic status, the disdain for labour and neglect of enterprise. 'As empire grew, so it aroused ambition, which gave way to greed, the root of all evils. ... Spain's ruin derived from its very greatness, which generated vices and excesses. Men became lazy, negligent of military discipline ... assuming that wealth and standing acquired through overseas expansion would sustain the monarchy', he observed.[41] Foreign intervention in Spanish life also played its part. Navarrete was hostile to the idea of immigration's being considered as a solution to Spain's demographic crisis and also warned against the potential risk of heresy, espionage and moral contagion that arose through commercial contact with non-Catholic countries. He referred to 'the transportation to our country of their vices, perversions, and luxuries, which has banished from Spain the thriftiness and temperance for which it once was praised ... It being certain that the presence of foreigners has introduced into Spain many household luxuries, and with them, many costly and effeminate wardrobes, in place of the important and traditional armouries.'[42]

Similarly, while he supported in principle the expulsion of the *moriscos* in 1609 so as to preserve the Catholic identity of Spain, he regretted the demographic and economic consequences and also acknowledged that the situation could have been avoided if the underlying issues had been dealt with differently. 'I am persuaded', he wrote, 'that, if we had found a means of granting [the Moriscos] some honour, without marking them with infamy ... they might have entered through honour's door into the temple of virtue, and obedience to the Catholic Church, without being incited to take contrary action.'[43] There is a subtle suggestion of ambivalence in Navarrete's judgement between the political and moral expediency which pervaded much commentary in the aftermath of the expulsion. Nevertheless, he accepted that, for all its reverses, Spain's religious policy, and the standing of the monarchy on the international stage that underpinned, it could not be compromised over and above other imperatives.[44]

Diego de Saavedra Fajardo (1584–1648), a distinguished Spanish diplomat at the court of Rome under Philip IV, wrote a manual for kingship in 1640, entitled *La Idea de un Príncipe-Político Cristiano*, translated into English in 1700 as *The Royal Politician*. It was addressed to the heir of the Spanish throne, Prince Baltasar Carlos (1629–46), and intended to guide him along the path of prudence – a quality that combined moral integrity with political skill – identified by Botero in his *Reason of State* as the master virtue of those entrusted with the exercise of leadership. In common with Botero, Saavedra sought to demonstrate that Christianity and politics could be reconciled in statecraft, contrary to Machiavellian teachings. Although he was somewhat removed from the traditional school of *arbitristas* and contemporary observers, Saavedra shared with them in acknowledging in his work the symptoms of Spain's economic decline and proposed reforms conducive to its recovery, as determined by the princples of Christian kingship that he advocated.[45] His work brings the cycle of commentary to a conclusion.

Saavedra, in accord with González de Cellorigo, pointed to the discovery of the American mines and the illusory sense of wealth this produced as the root cause of the downturn in Spain's fortunes. It had led to the neglect of agriculture and industry, the disdain of labour, monetary inflation and heavy borrowing to pay for debts. 'The scarcity of things in Spain', he observed, 'proceeds ... not from the infertility of the soil ... but this misfortune arrives from the neglect of husbandry, trades, business and commerce; the people, even the meanest of them, being so excessively proud, that they can't be content with what nature has given them, but aspire to something greater, loathing those employments which are not agreeable to their affected grandeur.'[46] In similar vein to Pérez de Herrera, he called for a policy of 'economic prudence', in response to Spain's crisis, that fostered a practical work ethic directed towards engagement in industry and commerce that would benefit the economy and to which all sectors of society would contribute. Following the advice of the Council of Castile, he also advocated a fairer tax system that would reduce the burden on the lower classes and raise the taxes levied on luxury items purchased by the elite. Together with Sancho de Moncada, he looked to the Church to help support the financial needs of the State and criticized the excessive number of feast days which took people away from their labours, the disproportionate growth of the religious orders, and those in university education, all of which contributed inversely to the economy. 'The Prince', he noted, 'should judiciously dispose the education of the youth, that the number of scholars, students and tradesmen be proportioned to his state. The same proportion should be observed in those that lead a monastic life, of whom too many is very prejudicial.'[47] Saavedra put forward pragmatic solutions to restore these imbalances: by working in harmony with one another, church and state could help to build a more prosperous society. However, as both he and Fernández de Navarrete witnessed at first hand, the practice of Christian statecraft in Habsburg Spain dictated that the interests of religion and reputation be prioritized at the expense of the exigencies of economic reform.

For all their endeavours, the reams of advice penned by the school of *arbitristas* were scarcely acted upon by their intended recipients – the king and his government. Although critcized for their exaggerations and for being out of touch with reality, some of these treatises are now recognized as offering a mature and often astute intellectual evaluation of the social, political and economic causes of Spain's decline that was not to resurface among native historians until the end of the twentieth century. In the intervening period, as we shall see, their work continued to provide an important reference point for scholars as they grappled with the phenomenon, to the extent that *arbitrista* theories constantly resurface in their discourses.

Notes

1 For an overview of the *arbitristas* and their philosophy, to which this chapter is indebted, see J.H. Elliott, 'Self-perception and decline in early seventeenth-century Spain', in *Spain and its World, 1500–1700* (New Haven, CT and London, 1989), pp. 241–61 and *The Count-Duke of Olivares*, pp. 89–94.
2 Martín González de Cellorigo, *Memorial de la política necesaria y útil restauración de la república de España y estados de ella y del desempeño universal de estos reinos*, ed. José L. Pérez de Ayala (Madrid, 1991), p. 95.
3 Sancho de Moncada, *Restauración política de España*, ed. Jean Vilar (Madrid, 1974), p. 105.
4 Elliott, 'Self-perception and decline', pp. 251–2.
5 Cited by Elliott, 'Self-perception and decline', p. 249.
6 Cited by Elliott, *The Count-Duke of Olivares*, p. 90.
7 Pedro Fernández de Navarrete, *Conservación de Monarquías y discursos políticos* (ed. Benito Cano, Madrid, 1792), Discurso XLIX, p. 409.
8 Peter Burke, 'Tradition and Experience: The Idea of Decline from Bruni to Gibbon', *Daedalus*, 105 (1976), 137–8.
9 Conrad Kent, 'Politics in *La hora de todos*', *Journal of Hispanic Philology*, 1 (1977), 99–100.
10 Marjorie Grice-Hutchinson, *Early Economic Thought in Spain, 1177–1740* (London, 1978), pp. 91–8.
11 Giovanni Botero, *The Reason of State*, translated by P.J. and D.P. Wayley (London, 1956); Robert Bireley, *The Counter-Reformation Prince. Anti-Machiavellianism or Catholic Statecraft in Early Modern Europe* (Chapel Hill, NC and London, 1990), pp. 51–6.
12 Botero, *Reason of State*, pp. 9–10.
13 Ibid., pp. 143–4.
14 Ibid., pp. 148–9.
15 Elliott, *The Count-Duke of Olivares*, p. 93.
16 Part of Martín González de Cellorigo's treatise is available in English translation in Jon Cowans (ed.), *Early Modern Spain. A Documentary History* (Philadelphia, PA, 2003), pp. 133–40.
17 González de Cellorigo, *Memorial de la política necesaria*, pp. 12–13, 21.
18 Ibid., p. 77.
19 Ibid., p. 90.
20 See L.P. Wright, 'The military orders in sixteenth- and seventeenth-century Spanish society', *Past and Present*, 43 (1969), pp. 34–70.
21 González de Cellorigo, *Memorial de la política necesaria*, p. 79.
22 Ibid., p. 160.
23 Ibid., p. 80.
24 Sancho de Moncada, *Restauración política de España*, p. 110.
25 Ibid., p. 111.
26 Ibid., p. 121.
27 Ibid., p. 162.
28 Ibid., p. 137.
29 Ibid., p. 160.
30 Ibid., p. 205.

31 Cristóbal Pérez de Ayala, *Amparo de los pobres* (Madrid, 1975), pp. 24–7, 39–40.

32 Ibid., p. 102.

33 Ibid., pp. 106, 108.

34 Anne J. Cruz, *Discourses of Poverty: Social Reform and the Picaresque Novel in Early Modern Spain* (Toronto, 1999), pp. 62–74.

35 A. González Palencia (ed.), *Archivo Histórico Español*, Vol. V (Valladolid, 1932), *La Junta de Reformación, 1618–1625*, doc. IV, *El Consejo Real a Felipe III*, 1 febrero 1619, pp.12–30 and Elliott, *Count-Duke of Olivares*, pp. 98–101.

36 Gonález Palencia, *Junta de Reformación*, p. 13.

37 Ibid., p. 16.

38 Ibid., p. 22.

39 Ibid., p. 25.

40 Ibid., pp. 27–8.

41 Pedro Fernández de Navarrete, *Conservación de Monarquías*, Discurso VIII, p. 84.

42 Ibid., Discurso XVII, pp. 135–6.

43 Ibid., Discurso VII, p. 72.

44 Michael D. Gordon, 'Morality, reform and the Empire in seventeenth-century Spain', *Il Pensiero Politico*, 11 (1978), 3–19.

45 Bireley, *The Counter-Reformation Prince*, pp. 188–216.

46 Diego de Saavedra Fajardo, *The Royal Politician represented in one hundred emblems*, translated by James Astry (London, 1700), Vol. 2, Emblem 71, p. 173.

47 Ibid., Emblem 66, p. 126.

3

The eighteenth century: enlightened opinion

No century has been more neglected by our historians [than the eighteenth], about none have we cared less, despite its nearness in time. ... Whenever we dabble in history, we run straight to our beloved fifteenth and sixteenth centuries, wherein lays our mythology. (Benito Pérez Galdós [1871], cited by Richard Herr, 'The twentieth century Spaniard views the Spanish Enlightenment', *Hispania*, 45:2 [May 1962], 183)

During the course of the eighteenth century, French writers and intellectuals assumed responsibility for transmitting the Enlightenment's values of individual freedom, reason and progress, which later acquired political dimensions, to other western European nations. Within this context, they constructed an image of Spanish decadence, derived from the old attitudes forged by the Black Legend, underpinned by anti-Habsburg sentiment, which was to become stereotypical for generations to come. In the absence of objective evidence and unable to see beyond the degenerate surface of Spain, French *philosophes* such as Montesquieu and Voltaire fell back on myth to define national characteristics. The liberal tradition was quick to judge that of the non-liberal unfavourably. As a result, a French representation of a Spain that had brought about its own ruin by virtue of its despotism and its unwillingness to embrace change in European thinking gained ascendancy. The prejudices and biases in their work prompted other scholars to look at Spain's predicament as a continuum of its seventeenth-century demise.[1]

The causes of Spain's decline as a nation, as well as being

examined by European economists, writers and philosophers, was for Spaniards themselves a crucial self-defining issue that exposed their cultural values and defined their political inclinations. In the context of the debate that followed, intellectuals such as Juan Pablo Forner refused to link their nation's decadence to defects in the Spanish character or an innate propensity to failure and called for greater historical awareness through which to defend their heritage and learn from the mistakes of the past. Liberal-minded reformers such as Pedro Rodríguez de Campomanes and Gaspar de Jovellanos sought to identify weaknesses in the structure of the economy, whose condition they attributed to the lack of political and scientific knowledge available in the seventeenth century. These deficiencies, they claimed, could be remedied in the eighteenth by a firmer intellectual grasp of economic matters that would in turn inform government policies and revive Spain's prosperity. These were to become the guiding principles of the internal reform programme. Change to the political system essentially lay outside their sphere of immediate concern.[2]

The writings of the French social commentator and political thinker Charles-Louis de Secondat, Baron de Montesquieu (1689–1755) provided a key test of the Enlightenment for those who were sceptical of its intentions. His arguments in favour of individual liberty, religious toleration and constitutional monarchy were far too progressive for the Inquisition, who banned his work. Montesquieu's theories on Spanish decadence were forged not through personal experience, but largely out of an acceptance of the old attitudes and prejudices propagated by Spain's Protestant enemies in the sixteenth century, which then became part of the conventional wisdom on the causes of its historical decline from power. 'There exist in Europe two extremes', he wrote in his private notebooks [Mes pensées], 'one of tolerance and one of intolerance. They are represented, on the one hand, by England [the model], and on the other, by Spain [the anti-model].'[3] Although it is true to say that Montesquieu was only partially in accord with the anti-Spanish bias that was typical among French enlightened thinkers, he nevertheless concurred with the majority view of his generation.

Montesquieu sought to understand the proper workings of government from a historical study of actual societies, undertaken in his most famous work, *De l'esprit des lois* [*The Spirit of Laws*] of 1748. He held that there were three types of government, each supporting a social principle: in a hereditary monarchy this was honour; in a democracy, virtue; and in a despotic government, fear.[4] He regarded Spain as the political anti-model whose development ran counter to the standard pattern of ebb and flow experienced by other nations, since, paradoxically, it fell into decline while it was at the height of its power. He therefore explained its weakness in terms of other deficiencies: its management of an overseas empire, the role of the Church and Inquisition and the character flaws of the Spanish people. Despite criticism of his work in Spain and its censorship at the hands of the Inquisition, most educated Spaniards in the 1780s would have acknowledged its importance in the field of political science and some may have had direct access to it.

Montesquieu borrowed from earlier political writers in suggesting that Spain's conquest and colonization of overseas territories had brought about its economic downfall. It had been led astray by the illusory qualities of gold and silver accumulation, which it mistook for real wealth. As a result, it failed to deploy its native resources to invest in commerce and industry and became dependent on foreign goods and loans to service its debts:

> Gold and silver are a wealth of fiction or of sign. ... The more they increase, the more they lose their worth, because they represent fewer things. When they conquered Mexico and Peru, the Spanish abandoned natural wealth in order to have a wealth of sign, which gradually became debased. ...There was soon double the silver in Europe, and the profit of Spain diminished in the same proportion. ... Spain resembles in her fate that foolish king to whom it was granted that all he touched turned into gold, and who then had to beg the gods that they put an end to his misery. ... The Indies and Spain are two powers under the same master, but the Indies are the principal one, and Spain is only secondary. In vain policy wants to reduce the principal one to a secondary one; the Indies continue to attract Spain to themselves.[5]

In common with earlier Black Legend literature, Montesquieu also pointed to the fanaticism engendered by the Spanish Church, evident since the expulsion of the Jews, the excessive powers and privileges invested in the ecclesiastical estate within what he described as a quasi-despotic governmental structure, as well as the repression exercised by the Inquisition, responsible for endangering peace and stability. In *The Spirit of the Laws*, he presented a 'Humble Exhortation to the Inquisitors of Spain and Portugal', which took the form of an imaginary plea for religious tolerance by a ten-year-old Jewish girl about to be burned in a Portuguese *auto de fe* and included a call for Spain to open itself up to natural reason. The reaction of the Inquisition was to prohibit the work:

> You live in a century when natural enlightenment is more alive than it has ever been, when philosophy has enlightened spirits, when the morality of your gospel has been better known, when the respective rights of men over each other … are better established. Therefore, if you do not give up your old prejudices, which, if you do not take care, are your passions, it must be admitted that you are incorrigible, incapable of enlightenment and of all instruction; and a nation is very unhappy that gives authority to men like you.[6]

Another leading figure of the French Enlightenment, Voltaire (François-Marie Arouet) (1694–1778), also used the Inquisition as a now familiar target of attack in his *Essai sur le moeurs et l'esprit des nations* [*Essay on the customs and spirit of nations*] of 1756, drawing attention to its excesses, its impact on the formation of the Spanish character and its assault on human liberty. Voltaire regarded the Spanish Inquisition, set in the context of European cultural history, as an embodiment of the fanaticism, bigotry and civil intolerance that had always existed in human societies but which took on a heightened significance in the context of the enlightened humanitarian philosophy he espoused. His critique, as that of Montesquieu, was largely derived from that of sixteenth-century Protestant polemicists and contributed to the dissemination of inquisitorial history founded on its propensity for abuse in the past rather than the present.

> The Popes set up inquisitorial tribunals for political reasons and Spanish inquisitors added their own brand of barbarism. … Torquemada was responsible for bringing a form of jurisdictional authority to the activity of the Spanish Inquisition that was in direct contravention of human law and which it still retains. … Its secret procedures made the whole of Spain tremble. Defiance took hold of Spaniards' spirits; the notion of friendship and society disappeared; brothers lived in fear of one another, just as a father of his son. From

then on silence became a characteristic of this nation, borne with all the vivacity inherent in a warm, fertile climate. ... We must also attribute to the Inquisition that deep ignorance of wholesome philosophy in which Spanish schools remain plunged whilst in Germany, France, England and even Italy so much truth was discovered and the sphere of our knowledge broadened. Never is human nature so debased as when superstitious ignorance is armed with political power.[7]

In his *Lettres persanes* [*Persian Letters*] – fictional tales of travel in eighteenth-century Europe – of 1721, Montesquieu drew associations between the Spanish character and the country's climate. He claimed that the intense heat made men passionate and violent. He also considered Spaniards to be naturally lazy and vain, characteristics which made them reluctant to engage in labour and promoted a false cult of nobility based on Old Christian ancestry. Their culture was backward and their own country a no man's land. His observations were, significantly, not drawn from first-hand evidence but replicated the account of a French traveller and writer, Madame D'Aulnoy, who had journeyed through Spain at the end of the previous century:

A man of such importance, a creature so perfect, would not go to work for all the treasure in the world, and could never bring himself to compromise the honour and dignity of his skin by degrading menial toil. ...You can find intelligence and sense among the Spaniards, but do not look for it in their books. If you saw one of their libraries, with romances on one side and scholastic philosophy on the other, you would say that the arrangement has been made, and put together to form a whole, by some secret enemy of human reason. ... They have made enormous discoveries in the New World, and do not yet know their own continent. There are bridges across their rivers which have not yet been discovered, and nations as yet unknown to them in their mountains. They say that the sun rises and sets in their territory, but it must be added that on its way it sees nothing but derelict countryside and empty wastes.[8]

As we have seen, Montesquieu's observations on Spanish decline were not entirely novel. The various themes that he drew together in his writing – the economic ruin of states, the refusal to embrace political liberty, the rejection of tolerance and the denial of natural law and reason – had their origins in the work of sixteenth-century writers and then resurfaced in the eighteenth in the context of enlightened analysis. His generalizations clearly did not take account of some of the preconditions of decline, notably Spain's pre-capitalist agricultural economy, nor the impetus to stimulate agriculture, industry, commerce as well as the arts and sciences promoted by enlightened reformers under Charles III (1759–88). Although educated Spaniards generally respected Montesquieu as a political scientist, the diffusion of anti-Spanish sympathies in his work, typical of Black Legend literature, understandably put them on the defensive. The prejudice of foreign writers provoked a passionate, nationalistic response. In 1782 the popular writer José Cadalso responded to Montesquieu's caricature of Spaniards, in his *Los eruditos a la violeta* [*The pseudo-scholars*] – a satirical attack on false scholars:

> That our nobility is born of idleness is a contradiction of history, not just that of Spain, but of Rome, France, Germany and many other countries. All the major noble houses of Spain were founded during the eight centuries of continuous bloody warfare with the Moors. ...
> While they [the Moors] had the support of the whole of Africa, our forefathers depended solely on love of their country and its religion. ... That our literature is based on novels and ecclesiastical texts is another falsity without foundation. Compare the dates of our literature with that of France where ancient languages, rhetoric, mathematics, navigation theology and poetry are concerned. ... Be aware of the danger of speaking badly about a foreign country you have never seen, especially when it possesses great talent, sound judgement, profound scholarship and a character that is respected in literary and political circles.[9]

In the same year, a little-known French writer, Nicolas Masson de Morvillers, launched a dramatic assault on Spain's intellectual and cultural credentials in an article on Spain printed in the *Encyclopédie Méthodique* [*Methodical Encyclopedia*] – a source of progressive ideas in the arts and science. It drew the conclusion that it was possibly the most ignorant nation in Europe and attributed this condition largely to the influence of the Inquisition, which epitomized everything against which the *philosophes* were struggling. The article soon became the quintessential statement concerning Spanish backwardness in the face of European progress:

The Spaniard has an aptitude for science and possesses many books and yet is perhaps the most ignorant of Europeans. What can one expect of a people who place so little value on reading and thinking? A book by a Protestant writer is banned by law, no matter what the subject matter, simply because of the religion of its author! All foreign literature is intercepted, subjected to scrutiny and a judgement is reached. Only if it is classified as light reading that does no harm to the spirit is it allowed into the country. ... If, on the contrary, it is a work of sound intellectual quality, it is burned for challenging the religion, way of life and good of the state. A book printed in Spain is regularly subject to six censures before being allowed to see the light of day and it is a wretched Franciscan friar or a barbarous Dominican who have the power to allow a man of letters to express his genius! ... But what has Spain done for us? After two, four, ten centuries, what has it done for Europe? Today it resembles one of those weak colonies who constantly have need of the protective arm of the mother country ... it can be compared to somebody who is desperately ill, but who is totally unaware of their malady and rejects the life support they are offered![10]

In response to this aggressive foreign criticism, Charles III ordered a ban on the import of the *Encyclopédie Méthodique* and demanded an official apology. As a form of counter-attack, the government encouraged responses to the charges made and the Spanish Academy offered a prize for the best 'apology or defence of the nation'. The winner was Juan Pablo Forner (1756–98), a friend and student of José Cadalso, who went on to pursue a career as a lawyer. In his prize-winning essay, *Oración Apologética por la España y su mérito literario* [*A speech in defence of Spain and its literary merits*] of 1786, he dismissed wholesale the intellectual achievements of the Enlightenment. 'Spain is surrounded by adversaries', he wrote, 'and the first is France. Her sophistry slanders Spain; and what are her arms? The first is ignorance.'[11] Expressing his unqualified admiration for the accomplishments of Spaniards in the traditional fields of law and theology, he contended that Spain possessed no need for a Descartes or a Newton. The country had already produced 'eminently just legislators and excellent practical philosophers who preferred the ineffable pleasure of serving the interests of humanity to the idle occupation of constructing imaginary worlds in the solitude and silence of a study'. He went on:

Men who scarcely know about our history, who have never read any of our literature, who are ignorant of our education system, who have no knowledge of our language, prized to speak about matters relating to Spain out of coincidence, instead of consulting appropriate sources to speak with authority, resort to the easier route of fiction and construct, at our expense, stories and fables that are so fanciful that they resemble the chivalric novels written by our ancient writers.[12]

The issue prompted a great debate in Spain in the late 1780s on how Spaniards should think about themselves, given what others thought about them. The majority of Spanish reformers opted for a middle way: rather than reject scientific knowledge, they sought to refocus attention on the intellectual endeavours of their contemporaries and their predecessors, including the economic tracts of the *arbitristas*. They thus embraced the discipline of history as a means of making sense of the present through the past.[13] Forner, in his *Discurso sobre el modo de escribir y mejorar la historia de España* [*Discourse on how to improve the writing of Spanish history*] (completed in 1788 and published in 1816), called for a fundamental revision in the writing of Spanish history:

> Until now our history has not been written with the necessary accuracy, serving instead to feed other peoples' interests and passions. Ferdinand the Catholic, Philip II and the great Duke of Alba provide notable examples in support of this observation. Foreign writers have cruelly blackened their reputation … digging them out of their graves in order to satirize those currently in power. If we were allowed to tell our own 'true' history not as eulogists but as judges, we would be able to reject foreign exaggerations. We would describe our ancestors exactly as they were and, at the same time, we would wipe away the falsities born of malice. But our lethargy as historians encourages foreigners to engage in telling stories that were invented two centuries ago to denounce our empire-building.[14]

Like Voltaire and other earlier historians, Forner believed that civilizations experienced growth, maturation and decay common to all living things. This 'cyclical theory' fell in line with the typical Spaniard's own interrogation of history and its application to the rise and decline of empires. Forner was the first Spanish historian to discredit the accomplishments of the Habsburg

period. He believed that Spain had fallen into decay when constitutional liberties were replaced by Habsburg absolutism. He called
for the writing of a dispassionate, new didactic history that would
not just glorify the personal feats of princes and statesmen, but
address the political life of the nation and the everyday concerns
of its people. The value of history when properly written was that
it could ensure a better future by exploring and reflecting on the
errors of the past:

> A king or minister who understands the causes that made his country
> great, those which ruined it, the means which other countries used to
> weaken it; those means which their ancestors used to sustain it; the
> motives which successfully have influenced legislation, the abuses
> introduced by ignorance or neglect which tyrannise over the
> economy and internal constitution, will know what to restrain, what
> to promote, what to moderate, what to alter, what to correct, and
> what to attend to within and without his estates.[15]

He considered one of the greatest obstacles to progress was ignorance. The regeneration of Spain called for the education of the
nation and the instilling of new values throughout society. 'We
want commerce, yet we scorn the merchant. We want agriculture
yet we despise the farmer. We praise lavishly the cloth from
England while we refuse to speak to the cloth manufacturer,'[16] he
wrote. Forner, while an implacable defender of Spanish culture in
response to foreign attacks, also played an important role in
formulating historical attitudes and critical techniques that would
influence the first generation of liberal-minded historians who
succeeded him in the following century. He thus stood at the
crossroads of conservatism and liberalism in his contribution to
the historiography of Spain's decline.

The Enlightenment made its mark on Spain, but in ways that
were more practical than theoretical, inspired and directed by two
major figures of the administration of Charles III: Pedro
Rodríguez de Campomanes and Gaspar Melchor de Jovellanos –
the standard bearers of the enlightened tradition in Spain and
successors of the *arbitrista* generation. They both forged the use of
history as a tool to effect economic reform. Pedro Rodríguez de
Campomanes (1723–1802) was one of the great intellectuals of
his generation, who served the Bourbon state both as an official

(president of the Council of Castile, 1762; prime minister, 1783–91) and as a reformer. He drew his politico-economic philosophy from a range of sources, including the ideas of the Enlightenment. He admired the encyclopaedic works of the Benedictine monk and university professor Benito Gerónimo Feijóo y Montenegro (1676–1764), whose writing was aimed at reversing the intellectual backwardness of his country as a function of its decline and opening it up to the scientific and philosophical trends that were widespread in more advanced European countries, such as France. A later edition of Feijóo's nine-volume *Teatro crítico universal* [*Universal critical history*] (1726–39) was endorsed by Campomanes himself. Opposed to privilege in society and a supporter of free trade and the open market, Campomanes remained committed to absolute monarchy and the strengthening of the power of the State. He was essentially a pragmatist who looked for practical solutions to his nation's century-old problems through a close examination of its past. Along with other members of his generation, he was of the view that the decline of Spain derived from vested interests being prioritized over those of the ordinary citizen and the common good. The privileges afforded to the sheep-owners' organization (the *Mesta*) over agriculture, the influence exercised by the guilds over Spanish industry and the disproportionate power of the elite classes within society were all held responsible. Above all, Spain's decadence was attributed to its over-reliance on bullion to sustain its economy, which led to a decline in manufacturing industries and consequently to an over-dependence upon foreign imports and foreign loans to mitigate the effects of inflation. These principles informed his writing.

In his *Tratado de la regalía de amortización* [*Treaty on ownership of property rights*] of 1765, he condemned the amount of landed property being held by churches and religious institutions in perpetuity, common throughout Catholic countries, and the failure of governments to restrict the practice.[17] He proposed that rights of ownership of arable land be returned to the peasant farmer from the privileged sectors (including the Church, nobility and sheep owners' guild), as well as the removal of restrictions on the price and movement of grain. His plan amounted to a code of agrarian law, a project subsequently taken up by fellow reformer

Gaspar de Jovellanos later in the century. In his *Discurso sobre el fomento de la industria popular* [*Discourse on the development of popular industry*] of 1774, Campomanes called for a revitalization of local crafts, enterprises and industries within rural communities, sustained by means of an infrastructure of education and instruction provided by the *Sociedades de Amigos del País* [*Economic Societies of Friends of the Nation*] and financial support from benevolent patrons, free from the restrictive practices of the guilds. 'Nothing is more contrary to popular industry than the erection of guilds and privileged jurisdictions, which divide people into small societies often exempt from ordinary justice,'[18] he observed. For Campomanes, a general application to productive work by men, women and vagrants was the antidote to idleness – a frequent charge made against Spain by her enemies to account for her backwardness – and paramount for the prosperity of its subjects. 'A large population, all usefully employed, and an industry incessantly encouraged in all ways', he wrote, 'are the two certain bases of the expansion of a nation.'[19] By extension, he recommended that the social stigma attached to work, derived from its association with those of lesser status and impure Christian origins – embedded in Spanish society for generations and linked to its economic decline – should be eradicated: 'We also need to remove all sense of dishonour from labour and enable those who work to take up public offices for the Republic.'[20] A new labour ethic was to be incorporated in Spanish law in 1783, which permitted artisans such as blacksmiths, tailors, cobblers, joiners and the like to be eligible for holding public office, on production of evidence of their integrity and respectability, as well as to make a claim to noble status, thus removing three centuries of shame attached to work, derived from the old elitist principles that had governed Spanish society for generations and impeded its progress.[21]

Campomanes supported the aims of the newly established Royal Academy of History (1738) to 'cultivate history in order to purify and clean inventions that mar our Spain'[22] and rose to become its director (1764–91). He favoured the use of critical methods and original source material in the writing of history, in accordance with developments in European historiography. He encouraged the writing of provincial histories, fostered by the

Economic Societies, as well as modern analyses of Spain's decline. Along with other contemporaries, he believed in the practical value of history and that evidence from the past would serve to inform the present. Eighteenth-century Spaniards, in the absence of comprehensive works of modern scholarship, relied to a large extent on the theories of earlier native historians, as well as works by foreign political economists. They looked back to the Habsburg era as a time when Spain's reputation as a nation, its internal stability and economic prosperity were seriously damaged by the impact of imperial policies. Campomanes drew many of his ideas from a critical reading of seventeenth-century *arbitristas* such as Cristóbal Pérez de Herrera, Pedro Fernández de Navarrete and Francisco Martínez de la Mata, whose treatises he edited and republished, as well as the work of the eighteenth-century theorist Gerónimo de Uztáriz, who advocated state intervention to develop industry and commerce along English and French lines.[23] In a real sense he tried to implement as policy what his ancestors had merely discussed as solutions to Spain's decline, as he himself acknowledged:

> The ancient economists (*arbitristas*), although inconsistent in their principles, deposited in their works an incredible number of facts, calculations, and arguments, as excellent as they are indispensable for a knowledge of the civil state of the nation and the influence of her political errors. There was lacking only an assiduous and wise hand to select through them and bring to light the true principles. The indefatigable magistrate [Campomanes], read and abridged these works, published the inedited, unearthed the unknown, made comments, rectified the opinions and corrected the reasoning of their authors. Improved by new and admirable observations, he presented them to his compatriots ... and the light of economics spread.[24]

Campomanes believed that the key to reversing Spain's fortunes lay in implementing a policy of free trade to counteract the detrimental effects of the mercantilist policies of previous reigns. Beyond its economic objectives, the principle of free trade also carried the potential to transform the whole framework of society. 'To extend to a people the liberty which prudence demands is the soul of commerce and of the happiness of the nation,'[25] he wrote to the Count of Llerena in 1790. Free trade meant political liberty, along the lines of that enjoyed in Britain and France, and the opening up of the American market to all subjects of the Castilian Crown. But for most Spaniards, these liberal economic principles, attractive though they were, exposed them to the risk of returning to the chaotic system of commercial deregulation that operated under Charles V and of losing its political stability and cultural integrity by exposure to foreign influences. Although by the late eighteenth century Campomanes had won the battle of ideas for Spain's recovery, there was a shortage of collective will among the ruling classes to turn enlightened reform into practical policy.[26]

Gaspar Melchor de Jovellanos (1744–1811) was one of the sharpest social critics and zealous reformers of his generation in Spain who shared Campomanes' views on the origins of Spain's decline and the measures needed to save it from further ruin. A politician, poet, economist and historian, who read both English and French, he was in every respect an educator and patriot. Versed in the writings of the Scottish-born philosopher and political economist Adam Smith (1723–90) and his anti-mercantilist views, Jovellanos regarded England's industrial development as an essential model for Spain's future and conducted a long correspondence on the subject with Lord Holland, the British Ambassador in Madrid. He vividly contrasted Spain's industrial future with its exploitive colonial past in one sentence: 'Coal contains as many possibilities as gold and silver; the problem is the lack of capital, and that here we prefer ignorance to enlightenment.'[27] Following the lead taken by Campomanes, Jovellanos worked for the suppression of the closed and reactionary guild structure, which impeded manufacture, and its replacement by a system of open competition, which would foster variety and invention in production. 'Let us with one blow break the chains that oppress and weaken our industry and let us restore once and for all the liberty we desire, on which our hopes for prosperity and growth are pinned,'[28] he urged. He was irreconcilably set against the greed, privilege and excessive temporal power of the Spanish Church. He worked to limit the authority of the Inquisition, which he saw as a fundamental obstacle to cultural and economic progress and a key instrument of national decay, but recognized that the task of abolishing it altogether was politically impossible, since it was too deeply rooted in the fabric of society and the

Crown was not prepared to confront it head on. Instead he sought to strip it of its arbitrary powers to ban books, shifting the power of censorship to the Royal Council and bishops. (He was later denounced to the Inquisition for his attack on ecclesiastical property and entail, but his case was suspended, due to his influence at court.) Jovellanos saw the monarchy not as an instrument of oppression, as did French revolutionaries, but as a guarantor of liberties. In his *Elogio* [*Eulogy*] to Charles III following his death in 1788, he praised the Bourbon king as the veritable fount of all enlightened impulses. He had guaranteed 'the circulation of truth' and he had stimulated the spread of knowledge and 'sown the seeds of light in the nation', much of this being due to his wise and far-sighted endorsement of the policies of Campomanes and his support of the Economic Societies of Friends of the Nation. In common with other members of his generation, Jovellanos knew of the work of the *arbitristas* and drew upon their language and theories in his own treatises, but was conscious that their intellectual efforts to restore the Spanish monarchy to good health had fallen on sterile ground, contrary to how he perceived the reception that his own ideas attracted.

Together with fellow reformer Forner, Jovellanos was concerned about the state of historical studies in Spain and looked to it to advance reform programmes. In an address to the Royal Academy of History in 1780, he called for the proper study of legal and constitutional history, which would form part of a broad history of Spanish civilization and, of course, was a theme linked to civil liberty, which had, according to modernizers, been suppressed since the early sixteenth century and contributed to Spain's ruin.[29] He lamented the lack of such a national history capable of teaching Spaniards how to better understand themselves, their reverses and their successes, a task that the Academy could itself help to promote:

> One can hardly find anything which contributes to present a clear picture of the times which are described in our chronicles, annals, histories, compendia and memoirs. Everything which is noxious in the kingdom can be found ... wars, battles, commotions, famines, plagues ... But where is a civil history which explains the origin, progress, and mutations of our constitution, of our political and civil hierarchy, of our legislation, of our customs and our miseries?[30]

In the late 1780s, having been banished from the royal court, Jovellanos was commissioned by the Madrid Economic Society to write a plan for agrarian reform legislation to be submitted to the Council of Castile. He published the *Informe sobre la ley agraria* [*Paper on agrarian law*] in 1795, a work commonly considered as the most important politico-economic manifesto of the whole Spanish Enlightenment, which impressed the then prime minister, Manuel Godoy. It was a powerfully argued plea for the development of agricultural land as private property and for the abolition of aristocratic entail, clerical mortmain, as well as land held in common ownership, all of which Jovellanos believed had contributed to Spain's economic depression. Henceforth the fruits of the land should belong not just to the owner, but to small tenant farmers as well, leading to greater yields and profits:

> The state of cultivation has always conformed to the existing political situation of the nation and such has been its influence that neither the temperate, gentle climate, nor the excellent fertility of the land, nor its capacity to produce the most varied range of crops, nor its advantageous position vis-à-vis maritime commerce, in short no natural advantages have been powerful enough to overcome the impediments which this situation [has created] to block its progress. ... The backwardness of agriculture is essentially rooted in the laws that govern agricultural production which need to be reduced rather than increased in number.[31]

But for all his radicalism, Jovellanos, whose views were shared by other liberal intellectuals, including some members of the Church, was not a revolutionary. His advocacy of liberal economics was tempered by a concern for political stability.

While French *philosophes* maintained a consistent attack on Spain's cultural and intellectual orientation as symptomatic of its decline, the desire of eighteenth-century Spanish enlightened reformers, such as Pedro Rodríguez de Campomanes and Melchor Gaspar de Jovellanos, was to assess the problems besetting their nation and to develop a reform programme, informed by rational thought, and apply pragmatic solutions to restore it to greatness. To this end they borrowed from foreign writers and the new science of political economy emerging from northern Europe, and also made extensive use of seventeenth-century Spanish treatises on the subject of decline. These were both adapted to shape their analysis of Spanish decadence: one based essentially on the restoration of the power and authority of the monarchy, from which economic reform would ensue.[32] But within a short period of time, in the aftermath of the French Revolution and the Napoleonic invasions, enlightened theories would give way to a new liberal political framework and philosophy of ideas that fed into the on-going decline debate.

Notes

1 María Carmen Iglesias, 'Montesquieu and Spain: Iberian identity as seen through the eyes of a non-Spaniard of the eighteenth-century', in Richard Herr and John H.R. Polt (eds), *Iberian Identity: Essays on the Nature of Identity in Portugal and Spain* (Berkeley, CA, 1989), pp. 143–55; Paul Ilie, 'Exomorphism: Cultural bias and the French image of Spain from the War of Succession to the age of Voltaire', *Eighteenth Century Studies*, 9 (Spring 1976), 357–89.

2 Charles Jago, 'The eighteenth century economic analysis of the decline of Spain', in Paul Fritz and David Williams (eds), *The Triumph of Culture: 18th Century Perspective* (Toronto, 1972), pp. 335–51.

3 Cited by María Carmen Iglesias, 'Montesquieu and Spain', p. 145.

4 Montesquieu, *Spirit of the Laws* (1748), translated by Anne M. Cohler, Basia Carolyn Miller and Harold Samuel Stone (Cambridge, 1989), Book III.

5 Ibid., Part 4, XXII, pp. 393–6.

6 Ibid., Part 5, XIII, p. 491.

7 Cited by Ricardo García Cárcel, *La Leyenda Negra. Historia y Opinión* (Madrid, 1998), pp. 151–2.

8 Montesquieu, *Persian Letters* (1721), translated by C.J. Bates (Harmondsworth, 1973), Letter 78, pp. 155–7.

9 Cited by García Cárcel, *La Leyenda Negra*, pp. 155–6.

10 Ibid., pp. 158–9.

11 Cited by Jago, 'The eighteenth century economic analysis of the decline of Spain', p. 341.

12 Cited by García Cárcel, *La Leyenda Negra*, p. 160.

13 Jago, 'The eighteenth century economic analysis of the decline of Spain', pp. 340–3.

14 Cited by García Cárcel, *La Leyenda Negra*, p. 161.

15 Juan Pablo Forner, *Discurso sobre el modo de escribir y mejorar la historia de España* (Madrid, 1816), p. 143.

16 Cited by George L. Vásquez, 'The historians of nineteenth-century Spain' (PhD thesis, Columbia University, 1978), p. 44.

17 Richard Herr, *The eighteenth century revolution in Spain* (Princeton, NJ, 1958), p. 18.

18 Pedro Rodríguez de Campomanes, *Discurso sobre el fomento de la industria popular* (Madrid, 1774), p. 109.

19 Ibid., pp. 52–3.

THE DEBATE ON THE DECLINE OF SPAIN

20 Ibid., p. 119.
21 Decree published in W.N. Hargreaves-Mawdsely (ed. and trans.), *Spain under the Bourbons, 1700–1833: A Collection of Documents* (Columbia, SC, 1973), pp. 166–7.
22 Cited by Gonzalo Pasamar, *Apologia and Criticism. Historical Writing in Spain 1500–2000* (Bern, 2010), p. 46.
23 Jago, 'The eighteenth century economic analysis of the decline of Spain', p. 348.
24 Cited in ibid., pp. 343–4.
25 Cited by Antony Pagden, 'Heeding Heraclides: Empire and its Discontents, 1619–1812', in R. Kagan and G. Parker (eds), *Spain, Europe and the Atlantic World: Essays in Honour of John H. Elliott* (Cambridge, 1995), p. 328.
26 John Lynch, *Bourbon Spain, 1700–1800* (Oxford, 1989), pp. 258–61.
27 Cited by Hugh Thomas, 'Gaspar Melchor de Jovellanos', in Fundación Amigos del Museo del Prado (ed.), *Goya* (Barcelona, 2002), p. 120.
28 Cited by Ruth MacKay, *'Lazy, Improvident People'. Myth and Reality in the Writing of Spanish History* (Ithaca, NY and London, 2006), p. 149.
29 Herr, *The Eighteenth Century Revolution in Spain*, pp. 341–2.
30 Cited by C. Sánchez Albornoz, 'Jovellanos ante la historia', in *Españoles ante la historia* (Buenos Aires, 1969), p. 154.
31 Gaspar Melchor de Jovellanos, *Informe sobre la ley agraria* (1795), www.cervantesvirtual.com/obra-visor/informe-sobre-la-ley-agraria—0/html/, pp. 4–5 (accessed 12 June 2011).
32 Jago, 'The eighteenth century economic analysis of the decline of Spain', pp. 337–8.

4

The nineteenth century: liberalism and conservatism

> If the memory of past glories serves to comfort distressed spirits and raise thoughts to higher spheres than those contemplated by our present patriotism, historical reverses and misfortunes can render an even greater service, which is to teach how to avoid these disasters. (Antonio Cánovas del Castillo, *El Solitario y su tiempo*, pp.128–9, cited by George L. Vásquez, 'Cánovas and the Decline of Spain', *Mediterranean Historical Review*, 7:1 [1992], 73)

The beginning of the nineteenth century witnessed two events that impacted on historical discourse in general and the historiography of Spain's decline in particular. The first was the opening up of Spanish archives, although still devoid of order and indexes, to the general public and the emergence of new professional trends in the writing of history, stimulated by the work and ethos of Leopold von Ranke (1775–1886) and others. Ranke, a Protestant German and professor of history at the University of Berlin for almost half a century (1825–71), pioneered the use of original archival material to establish the true facts on which knowledge should be built and promoted the writing of history free from political and confessional bias and prejudice. It was necessary, as he put it, for the historian 'to extinguish [his] own self, as it were, to let the things speak and the mighty forces appear which have arisen in the course of centuries'.[1] For Ranke, the core tenets of historical enquiry involved the rigorous examination of evidence, verified by references, coupled with objective analysis. He argued that historians should refrain from judging the past according to their own criteria. The empirical research Ranke pioneered, there-fore, would be devoid of the beliefs and prejudices that had characterized the vigorously partisan discourse of the previous century and that passed as history. Factuality and objectivity thus became the two principles underpinning the claims that the new school of Rankean historiography made for itself.

Ranke's theories on historical writing also have to be under-stood in relation to the religious and political context in which they emerged, characterized by the breakdown in spiritual unity and the growth of nationalism within the European state struc-ture. These circumstances provided the second impetus for the rewriting of history and had particular repercussions for Spain. In the opening decades of the nineteenth century, the War of Independence (1808–14) witnessed the Spanish people rise up in resistance to Napoleon and, with considerable help from Britain, drive out French forces from the peninsula, creating the image to the outside world of a fiercely independent nation defending its land and its liberties. The approval of a new liberal constitution by a delegation of the revolutionary Cortes meeting at Cádiz (1810–13) appeared to herald the end of the old conservative order in Spain. Although it recognized Ferdinand VII as king, it claimed sovereignty ultimately resided with the Spanish nation (including inhabitants of Spain's overseas colonies) and its parlia-mentary representatives. The constitution dismantled the absolutist regime and the hierarchical order of society associated with it. It abolished seigniorial jurisdiction and fiscal privileges, gave all citizens equality before the law, provided for universal access to education and freedom of the press. It protected Catholicism as the official state religion but denounced the Inquisition. For all their revolutionary ideals and desire to replace arbitrary rule with a democratic system, liberals assembled at Cádiz could not count upon universal popular support for their agenda or prevent a conservative backlash.[2] The middle of the nineteenth century witnessed the failure of bourgeois liberalism and the collapse of constitutional monarchy, followed by the fragile alternation of progressive and moderate governments in power. Meanwhile, the instability that followed the Napoleonic invasions and the spread of liberal ideas – some of them enshrined in the Cádiz constitution – provided the opportunity for the

Spanish American colonies to seek their independence. By 1825, all former Spanish and Portuguese possessions in Latin America, with the exception of Cuba and Puerto Rico, had won their freedom from imperial control.

This period of profound political uncertainty prompted native historians to examine the roots of their nation's dilemma. Liberal interpretations, such as those of Juan Antonio Llorente and Modesto Lafuente, became embedded in Spanish historical discourse, tempered by the conservative responses of Marcelino Menéndez y Pelayo and Antonio Cánovas del Castillo, mirroring both the political climate of the times as well as the on-going debate between scholars of differing ideological outlooks on Spain's historical development. Meanwhile, foreign historians such as William Prescott and Henry Charles Lea took an interest in the neglected history of Spain, encouraged by their access to new source materials. One of the most tangible outcomes of these events for nineteenth-century Spanish historiography was that the Inquisition, whose role in shaping society lay at the heart of the whole decline debate, came under critical scrutiny for the first time, and from within.

Juan Antonio Llorente (1756–1823), an ordained priest who worked first as a fiscal secretary to the bishop of Burgos, then as a commissioner for the tribunal of the Inquisition located in Logroño (1785) and subsequently as secretary of the Supreme Council of Inquisition (the *Suprema*) in Madrid (1789–91), was a seminal figure in the emergence of this new history. In the 1790s he entered the service of Manuel Godoy, the enlightened minister of Charles IV, whose political persuasions he shared, and became exposed to the prevailing criticisms of excessive ecclesiastical privilege and authority in society. Three years later, at the request of the reform-minded and progressive Inquisitor General Manual Abad y La Sierra, he began writing a series of essays on the Holy Office with a view to reforming its practices, which won him favours at court. He subsequently used the opportunity afforded by the French invasions of Spain (1808–14) and the liberal reforms that ensued (including the temporary abolition of the Holy Office following the majority vote of the Cortes in 1813) to write a 'true' history of the Inquisition, based on his own experience and personal access to its secret archives, sequestered by

Joseph Bonaparte in 1808. These 'first hand' sources had never previously been freely available for research purposes, even to Catholic historians, who had to rely on official documentation written with an apologetic bias to produce their narratives. Much of the myth and propaganda that built up around the Inquisition's reputation derived from a lack of factual knowledge and objective study of its practices. What made Llorente stand out was his position as the first internal employee of the Holy Office to write a critical history of its operations using original evidence.

Llorente worked continuously on the Inquisition's records from 1808 to 1813. The following year saw the return of Ferdinand VII to the Spanish throne and the re-establishment of the Holy Office. Llorente left for France, where he wrote his most celebrated work, *Histoire Critique de l'Inquisition d'Espagne* [*Critical History of the Spanish Inquisition*], published in self-imposed exile in Paris in 1817. It was soon translated into several languages, including Spanish in 1822 (*Historia Crítica de la Inquisición Española*), prompting a fierce backlash from the Inquisition's defenders, swiftly followed by Llorente's excommunication from the Catholic Church a year later. In the introduction to his work Llorente wrote:

> Although a tribunal has existed for more than three hundred years in Spain, invested with the powers of prosecuting heretics, no correct history of its origin, establishment, and progress has been written. . . . I feel that the tribunal merits its own history, one that does not attempt to hide or exaggerate the facts . . . or present anything other than the truth about its secret laws and activities . . . While I was a secretary of the Inquisition at Madrid, during the years 1789, 1790, and 1791, I got to know its workings in depth to be firm in my conviction that it was evil in principle, in its constitution and its laws, notwithstanding all that has been said in its support. Since then I have dedicated myself to collecting every document I could procure relative to its history . . . so as to fill in the gap in this field of literature and satisfy public knowledge.[3]

Llorente made judicious use of inquisitorial documents, including case studies, procedural manuals and internal correspondence, as well as official histories and chronicles to compile his *Historia Crítica* and adopted a strong polemical tone in identifying those areas where the Inquisition's impact had been detrimental to

Spain's development. Although he was forced into exile in 1813, it is very likely that his ideas influenced the deliberations of the Cortes of Cádiz, where liberal delegates such as Antonio Puigblanch made powerful speeches in which they bitterly condemned the Inquisition as the embodiment of all the evils of the Old Regime – ignorance, intellectual stagnation and fanaticism – and held it responsible for the nation's decline.[4] The Spanish artist and liberal sympathizer, Francisco de Goya (1746–1828), also took up Llorente's theme in his series of dramatic images of victims of inquisitorial abuse, collected in his Album C, executed as the Holy Office was reinstated in 1814 (Figures 4 and 5). The *Historia Crítica* confirmed the anomalies and corruption inherent in the Inquisition's methods that foreign writers alluded to but had no real evidence to support. It also attempted to evaluate the impact of the Holy Office on social minorities, intellectual life and the economy. Llorente pointed to the failure of the Church to provide *conversos* and *moriscos* with adequate religious instruction as a factor that led them to revert to the practice of their old faith. 'The Inquisition encouraged hypocrisy, punishing only those who knew no better or would not yield; but it converted nobody. The Jews and Moors who were baptized without being truly converted, merely that they might remain in Spain, are examples that prove the truth of this assertion,'[5] he observed. He criticized the Inquisition for inhibiting the development of the arts, industry and trade: 'The horrid conduct of this holy office weakened the power and diminished the population of Spain, by arresting the progress of arts, sciences, industry, and commerce, and by compelling multitudes of families to abandon the kingdom.'[6] He also condemned inquisitors for being motivated by financial greed rather than the imposition of religious uniformity: 'Facts prove beyond a doubt, that the extirpation of Judaism was not the real cause, but the mere pretext, for the establishment of the Inquisition by Ferdinand and Isabella. The true motive was to carry out a vigorous system of confiscation against the Jews, and so bring their riches into the hands of the government.'[7] He argued that the Spanish Inquisition had exceeded the limits of its authority, leading to the practice of abuse that ran contrary to Christian teachings. He proposed that it should therefore be divested of its powers and its responsibilities be returned to the

Church. In essence, he claimed, 'the tribunal could not preserve its claim to being just if it continued to use the methods of three centuries past'.[8] For all his critical observations, Llorente did not attempt anything approaching a full empirical study. Nor could he claim to be detached from the political agenda. Llorente's work was utilized by liberals to validate the familiar arguments surrounding the Inquisition, regarded as the symbolic shorthand of all that was deemed to be wrong with Spain, as evidenced in its resistance to embrace the Enlightenment and failure to progress into the modern era. Outside Spain where his work was soon published in Italian (1820), Dutch (1821), German (1823) and English (1826) translation, his interpretation linked to the progressive standpoint in a similar way to that in which Bartolomé de Las Casas' *Brief Account of the Destruction of the Indies* had helped to endorse anti-Catholic opinion two hundred and fifty years earlier. Nevertheless, the impact of the *Historia Crítica* on nineteenth-century Spanish historiography was considerable, leading to a better understanding of the Holy Office as a symbol of darker times in Spain's past that had no relevance to the future.[9] The wide dissemination of Llorente's work in the 1820s and the questions it raised coincided with the beginning of the Inquisition's permanent disestablishment as an institution and may even have hastened it. Only then could a revised, fully objective assessment of its contribution to the nation's decline really begin.

Beyond the work of Llorente, liberalism as a school of historiography emerged in the first half of the nineteenth century through the writing of the Spanish essayist and journalist turned historian, Modesto Lafuente (1806–66), who produced the first general history of Spain since the Jesuit historian Juan de Mariana published his *Historiae de rebus Hispaniae* in 1592.[10] Lafuente's thirty-volume *Historia General de España* (1850–67) filled a major gap in national historical literature that would reawaken the public's interest in history (the absence of which had been lamented by intellectuals in the previous century) and launch a new historiographical era in Spain. However, the weakness of his work lay in its subjectivity. In setting forth a liberal interpretation of Spain's past, he rejected the Habsburg legacy, heralding it as a two-hundred year period of decadence when ancient liberties were suppressed through the introduction of state centralism, the

Figure 4 Francisco de Goya, *Muchos an acabado así* [Many have ended up like this], c.1814–24. Museo Nacional del Prado, Madrid

Figure 5 Francisco de Goya, *Pr linage de ebreos* [For being of Jewish ancestry], c.1814–24. © Trustees of the British Museum

growth of religious intolerance was promoted through the tyrannous hand of the Inquisition and Spain's resources were drained by ruinous foreign policies. By contrast, Lafuente referred to the eighteenth century as a period when 'the enlightened men of the nation took advantage of the great popular movement to regenerate Spain politically ... labouring to erect the edifice of Spanish freedom',[11] a process consolidated at the beginning of the nineteenth century in the 'triumph' of constitutionalism. Spanish liberal history, as espoused by Lafuente, for all its professional endeavours, was essentially partisan history that promoted the rise of reason over obscurantism and was unable to divorce itself from the political and ideological controversies of the times. By adopting such a pronounced bias, liberal historians invited their conservative counterparts to contest their charges with their own brand of rhetoric, and so perpetuated the debate over the 'Two Spains' that so distorted the historiographical record.

Marcelino Menéndez y Pelayo (1856–1912) was the principal standard bearer of learned conservatism in nineteenth-century Spain and, arguably, the most important figure in the history of ideas at the time. On the basis of his intellectual prowess, he was elected to a professorial chair at the age of 21 and later became director of the Spanish National Library. To appreciate Menéndez y Pelayo's contribution to historiography and the on-going debate between historians over Spain's past, present and future to which he contributed, one has to understand the importance of his philosophy and Catholic faith to his historical vision.[12] He wrote in a period of political turmoil and ideological polarization in Spain's history that led to disillusion and despair over its future direction. Menéndez y Pelayo sought consolation in the glories and achievements of Spain's golden age which rested on the strength of its Catholic unity and the success of its providential mission, both of which were absent in the present. 'The lustre of Spain in the sixteenth century', he observed, 'was due not to its victories on the battlefield, nor to its power, nor to its predominance over the rest of the world, it was due to the formidable enterprise of Christianising the Renaissance and disseminating its culture through the world.'[13] He yearned for the resurgence of traditional Spain and unashamedly promoted its values through the writing of history. In common with Forner in the previous century, Menéndez y Pelalyo believed that the role of the historian was to appreciate why events had occurred in the past in order to apply their lessons to the present. The study of history, therefore, was far from being an irrelevant issue. In his view, a nation that disregarded its history neglected its own destiny, and by extension its divine purpose, which he saw as the primary force behind change in history. He perceived the role of the mid-nineteenth-century Spanish historian as being to restore to Spain an acute awareness of its historical identity and to use this as a focus for national regeneration.

Menéndez y Pelayo's work also needs to be placed in the context of historical studies in late nineteenth-century Spain.[14] Advances in historical scholarship in other western European countries had barely made an impact inside Spain. Although Spanish history had begun to emerge as an academic discipline by mid-century, publication was limited to general histories, such as that of Lafuente, and collections of sources, rather than their critical analysis. There was little or no evidence of a commitment to original archival investigation, nor did historians attempt to disguise their partisanship. Catholic historiography was essentially retrospective, invoking the past as a source of inspiration for the present, while its liberal counterpart aimed at rescuing Spain from foreign hostility and myth making and celebrating its progressive achievements. Both liberals and conservatives made use of Spanish history for their own ends. While the former attributed Spain's decadence to its exclusive religious policies, the latter clung to it as a source of inspiration.[15] The philosophy that Menéndez y Pelayo espoused in this work – that nothing could be more alien to Spain's national identity than heterodox views – naturally appealed to the right wing and, following his death, was embraced by his devotees as a weapon in the ideological struggle against the Republic in the Spanish Civil War.[16] In 1930s Spain he was hailed as a prophet and liberator, a champion of the notion of 'Hispanidad' (a term used to celebrate the racial and cultural superiority of Hispanic Catholic nations) with a message for modern Spain. His interpretation of Spanish history as a spiritual mission that embodied the values of the homeland and underpinned all its imperial achievements became a formal part of the secondary-level history syllabus in Spanish schools from 1939.[17] Despite his partisan views and the controversy they aroused, he did much for Spanish historical studies, advocating the need to return to the sources of Spanish history in order to rebuild knowledge and dispel national ignorance.

In 1876 he wrote *La Ciencia Española* [*Spanish Science*], an attack on enlightened criticism of Spain's intellectual backwardness, in which he took issue with those who attributed all national defects, including religious intolerance and lethargy, to the activities of the Inquisition:

> This terrifying name of Inquisition, a bogey-man for infants and a menace for adults, is for many the solution for all our problems, a 'deus ex machina' which arrives unexpectedly in dangerous situations. Why was there no industry in Spain? On account of the Inquisition. Why are there bull-fights in Spain? On account of the Inquisition. Why do Spaniards take a siesta? On account of the Inquisition.[18]

He turned the argument on its head by suggesting that the Inquisition was not a cause of intolerance but an effect, resulting from the racial tensions provoked by the Jews and their descendants. He strenuously denied that the Inquisition had systematically persecuted intellectuals, wiping out literature and learning from Spain. Rather, poets, philosophers, political theorists, jurists and theologians flourished during this period but remained virtually unknown outside Spain.

> Never have writers written on more subjects with greater authority in Spain than during these two golden centuries of the Inquisition. That this fact was not known by the delegates who sat at the Constituent Cortes of Cádiz, nor by their sons or grandsons, is also nothing unusual ... Why should they read books? It is much more convenient to deny their existence.[19]

Menéndez y Pelayo's major work, *Historia de los Heterodoxos Españoles* [*History of Spanish Heterodoxy*] (1880–82), was written in part to refute Llorente and Puigblanch's attacks on the institution that in his view was central to Spanish nationhood, and also to explore the controversial subject of religious dissidence ('the history of Spain seen upside down', as he referred to it), which had been largely neglected by native historians. He identified Spaniards as God's chosen people whose racial and cultural purity was threatened by exposure to heterodox influences, and that hence was obliged to defend itself via the activities of the Holy Office. For Menéndez y Pelayo, the Inquisition was a fundamental instrument of the Catholic state and personified the beliefs and conscience of the Spanish people. By separating out the faithful from the non-faithful, it strengthened the religious unity of the Spanish kingdoms and, by extension, their political cohesion. Spain's decadence as a nation, in his view, was due to the infiltration of alien values and the growth of secularism that permeated society during the eighteenth century and threatened its Catholic identity. Herein lay the essential tenets of the White Legend which Menéndez y Pelayo, above all other Spanish historians, encapsulated in his work.

The statesman-turned-historian, Antonio Cánovas del Castillo (1828–97), was arguably the most important nineteenth-century Spanish historian to address the phenomenon of Spain's decline, publishing three major works on the subject between 1854 and 1888: *Historia de la decadencia de España desde el advenimiento de Felipe III al trono hasta la muerte de Carlos II* [*History of the Decline of Spain from the succession of Philip III to the death of Charles II*] (1854); *Bosquejo histórico de la Casa de Austria en España* [*A historical sketch of the House of Austria in Spain*] (1868) and *Estudios del reinado de Felipe IV* [*A study of the reign of Philip IV*] (1888).[20] He was also a distinguished conservative politician who supported the restoration of the Bourbon monarchy from 1875 and instituted a framework of political conciliation with liberal opponents. He served as prime minister for six terms between 1845 and 1897, meeting his death at the hands of an anarchist assassin during his final period of tenure. As director of the Royal Academy of History from 1875, he played a key part in promoting historical research and scholarship among academicians (a role not taken up by universities until the following century). Cánovas took an interest in the history of Spain's decline under the Habsburgs at a time when it was a highly unfashionable area of research and had effectively remained a dormant subject with Spanish scholars. While he understood why native historians had chosen to neglect the seventeenth century, he believed that this had been to their disadvantage, since they had allowed foreigners to take over the territory and impose their own negative bias on Spain's demise, leading to the creation of a national inferiority complex. Furthermore, by choosing to acknowledge only their nation's greatness, and not its misfortunes, they were failing to accept the didactic lessons of history that were directly relevant to their current predicament. Although essentially conservative in his judgements, Cánovas injected a new sense of professionalism into the writing of Spanish history, informed by a deductive reading of the past, attempting to exonerate his nation's reputation under the Habsburgs while accepting its failures.

The essential premise of Cánovas' argument was that Spain's imperial greatness in the seventeenth century was eclipsed by the over-extension of its resources and economic weakness, rather than by the failings of its monarchs, ministers or institutions, frequently cited as the principal causes of its decline. In this respect, Spain was not so different from other countries. 'Our old institutions were not perfect, just as they were imperfect elsewhere; nor have those who have ruled us all been honourable and great men, a felicitous condition which no nation has ever attained,'[21] he observed. The major error of the Habsburgs had been to commit to maintaining an empire that was far beyond its military and administrative means, leading to bankruptcy, dependence on foreign loans and ultimately military defeat. 'In the long run', he wrote, 'the permanent state of deficit was a thousand times more doleful for Spain than the Inquisition.'[22]

He felt that the economic backwardness of Spain, a legacy that still haunted it in the nineteenth century, was central to its collapse, but was not due solely to poor understanding or management of the economy. While the discovery of instant wealth in the New World played its part in the neglect of enterprise, so too did the rise of the northern European economies of England, France and Holland, which far surpassed that of Spain in terms of their efficiency and output. By contrast, Spaniards, 'without great interest in industry, without means of competing successfully in the market place, with abundant gold and the expectation of always having it and each day in greater amounts, almost completely abandoned the path [of economic development]'.[23] Additionally, Cánovas felt that too little attention had been placed by historians on the shortage of native manpower available to sustain the Spanish economy and promote an industrious spirit – a shortage resulting from the expulsion of religious minorities, the colonization of the Americas and military recruitment. He had no qualms about pointing the finger of blame at the Spanish aristocracy for failing to set an example for the rest of society. 'Spain's ruling class in the seventeenth century', he noted, 'like all others is held responsible by history for the decline, ignorance and selfishness of the masses, because it is obliged to be their model and guide.'[24]

Despite his conservative credentials and the importance he attached to the role of the Catholic Church in protecting Spain from the heretical influences of the Protestant Reformation, Cánovas did not shy away from highlighting the Inquisition's negative influence on Spain's historical development, even going as far as to call for its abolition. By generating religious intolerance, fostering fanaticism and repressing learning, it deeply set back the nation's progress and exercised an excessive intrusion into all aspects of life:

> The Inquisition went ahead in the fashion of a serpent, twisting itself menacingly around the body of Spanish thought until, during the reign of Philip II's successors, it tightened its grip to such an extent that it suffocated it, causing its death. [...] While in the other nations of Europe, new fertile ideas, born from the heat of arguments and freedom of thought, revealed useful discoveries which developed human progress in a vigorous and glorious fashion.[25]

Where his assessment of Habsburg kingship is concerned, Cánovas, an advocate of monarchy as one of the central pillars of the Spanish political system, drew a clear distinction between the greater reputations of sixteenth-century rulers and the lesser standings of their seventeenth-century counterparts, and by so doing gave the rise-and-decline phenomenon a clearly defined time-frame. He portrayed Philip II as the first modern European statesman, who stood at the threshold of Spain's greatness and decay. The practice of despotism and tyranny with which Spain's enemies associated his rule were, argued Cánovas, traits common to other sovereigns of the age. He characterized Philip III as a good Catholic but a poor ruler who allowed greed and venality to contaminate the administration, while he judged Philip IV to be disinterested in his duties as king. Cánovas undertook a major reassessment of the Count-Duke Olivares, first minister of Philip IV, much maligned by history. He considered him to be a statesman of immense talent who dedicated himself with unswerving energy to the daunting task of reversing Spain's ailing foreign, domestic and economic fortunes but who might have achieved greater success had he pursued more modest policies. Under the later Habsburgs, Cánovas observed, Spain failed to regenerate itself and deteriorated into a passive, fatigued nation, opposed to change and resigned to its fate.

However, Cánovas was not a prophet of doom. He believed strongly in the resurgence of nations, echoing the firm belief of conservative historiography in the historical mission of Spain and the resilience of its people: 'That which made a great Spain possible still exists in latent form. There is something in our nation which has never decayed nor can ever decay: [the Spanish] race.'[26] Like his contemporary Menéndez y Pelayo, Cánovas felt that nineteenth-century Spaniards could learn lessons from their nation's historic rise and fall that would help them to build a more prosperous, stable future, tempering their aspirations to the reality of their condition. Cánovas' theories on the decline of Spain, although conservative by definition, began to steer a course away from the 'Two Spains' debate and towards a more measured understanding of the past that the next generation of Spanish scholars would build upon in their research.

American scholarship also informed the nineteenth-century debate on Spain's past, a trend that was to add a new dimension to the historiography of its decline. John Lothrop Motley (1814–77) was a New Englander of vast learning and abilities. He graduated from Harvard at the age of 17 and went on to study law and literature in Germany. After a period of travel he settled down to practise law in Boston, but soon turned his attention to historical studies. In the 1840s he began to plan the writing of a history of the Netherlands, choosing to focus on the period relating to the United Provinces' struggle to attain independence from Spanish rule, which bore similarities to the history of the United States. He saw both nations as having achieved freedom against the forces of despotism and oppression. In the early 1850s he worked in the archives of Dresden, Brussels and the Hague and went on to publish the first volume of his *The Rise of the Dutch Republic* in 1856, which was well received and translated into several languages. It was followed by his *History of the United*

Netherlands, completed in 1867. Despite his experience in Germany, Motley was not influenced by the new school of Rankean historical research. Instead he wrote didactic history in a stirring style that clearly reflected his own personal prejudices. He made no attempt to disguise his sympathy for the Dutch in their struggle for independence and portrayed Philip II, from a stern Protestant moralist perspective, as the embodiment of tyranny and cruelty and the architect of Spain's demise as a nation:

> The causes of what is called the greatness of Spain are not far to seek. Spain was not a nation, but a temporary and factitious conjunction of several nations, which it was impossible to fuse into a permanent whole, but over whose united resources a single monarch for a time disposed. And the very concentration of these vast and unlimited powers, fortuitous as it was, in this single hand ... impelled him to those frantic and puerile efforts to achieve the impossible, which resulted in the downfall of Spain. The man who inherited so much material greatness believed himself capable of destroying the invisible but omnipotent spirit of religious and political liberty in the Netherlands, of trampling out the national existence of France and of England, and of annexing those realms to his empire. It has been my task to relate ... how miserably his efforts failed. [...] There have been few men known to history who have been able to accomplish by their own exertions so vast an amount of evil as the king [Philip II].[27]

Motley's history of the United Netherlands was a classic expression of the anti-Spanish, anti-Catholic attitudes typical of Black Legend literature that continued to exert an influence on the historiography of Spain's decline into the nineteenth century.

William Hickling Prescott (1796–1859) – possibly the most prolific writer of his generation – produced four major histories of early modern Spain and its empire in the first half of the nineteenth century: *History of the Reign of Ferdinand and Isabella* (1837), *History of the Conquest of Mexico* (1843), *History of the Conquest of Peru* (1847) and *History of the Reign of Philip II* (1855). After graduating from Harvard, Prescott studied European literature before turning his hand to the writing of Spanish history. He wrote for a general readership in an accessible, flowing style (similar in many ways to Macaulay's in England) and wanted his books – written with the handicap of failing eyesight – to be enjoyable as well as useful. He sought to interpret the facts of history in such a way as to make them both appealing, by adopting an epic style, and instructive, incorporating a principled message. Prescott thus touched upon what he felt were the weaknesses of the likes of Voltaire and Gibbon, whose histories were, in his judgement, 'nowhere warmed with generous moral sentiment'. No American scholar before him had attempted to use original documents – including state papers, reports of ambassadors and contemporary chronicles obtained via friends and contacts – following the approach of Ranke, to write a new, narrative-style history with 'philosophical' reflections about another nation, underpinned by a commitment to accurate, sound scholarship. In accordance with his sources and method, Prescott recorded the making of history from above, with an emphasis on monarchy, diplomacy and empire. His works proved to be very popular and for well over a century played a decisive role in shaping the character and direction of early modern Spanish historical scholarship, both in America and beyond.[28]

One of Prescott's aims was to determine the forces that destined certain societies for greatness – for which he used the American model – and others to decadence and decay, citing the case of Spain. Although he did not set out to denigrate Spain's Catholic tradition in his work, as did other nineteenth-century scholars such as his friend John Motley, and was essentially well disposed towards Spain, Prescott's arguments were nevertheless coloured by his Protestant Unitarian sympathies, typical of his generation, which determined his interpretation of events. His reading of Spain's rise and decline, defined by his liberal background, was also heavily influenced by enlightened scholarship of the previous century, which drew upon the presuppositions of the Black Legend. Prescott held the Habsburg monarchy responsible for crushing liberty and enterprise, leading to economic backwardness and intellectual stagnation, together with moral decay. He highlighted religious bigotry and political despotism as the two fundamental weaknesses of Spain's historical trajectory under the Habsburgs, and which became most destructive under Philip II. He observed that the king 'ruled over [the empire] with an authority more absolute than that possessed by any European prince since the days of the Caesars'[29] and that his policies reduced Spain to a state of indolence that led directly to its progressive decline.

Moreover, his rigid adherence to orthodoxy prompted the monarch to seek recourse in the repressive force of the Inquisition to ensure that the Catholic identity of his monarchy was maintained intact. Essentially, Prescott deemed Philip culpable, via the activity of the Holy Office, of preventing Spain from embracing the liberty and progress associated with the modern, free world. Here his interpretation clearly borrows from the enlightened critique of his sources:

> Spain might now boast that the stain of heresy no longer defiled the hem of her garment. But at what price was this purchased? Not merely by the sacrifice of the lives and fortunes of a few thousands of the existing generation, but by the disastrous consequences entailed forever on the country. Folded under the dark wing of the Inquisition, Spain was shut out from the light which in the sixteenth century broke over the rest of Europe, stimulating nations to greater enterprise in every department of knowledge. This genius of the people was rebuked, and their spirit quenched, under the malignant influence of an eye that never slumbered, of an unseen arm ever raised to strike. How could there be freedom of thought, where there was no freedom of utterance? Or freedom of utterance, where it was dangerous to say too little as to say too much? Freedom cannot go along with fear. Every way the Spanish mind was in fetters.[30]

At the same time, and as first pointed out by seventeenth-century commentators, Prescott acknowledged that the signs of decay coincided with the accession of the Habsburg monarchy in the sixteenth century and therefore were not exclusively a seventeenth-century phenomenon. It was this 'golden age' that witnessed Spain's subjection to the demands of empire and loss of liberty, on account of the absolutist pretensions of its rulers, beginning with Charles V. He thus exposed one of the great paradoxes of the rise-and-decline phenomenon: as the nation reached the highest point of its prosperity and world dominion – 'the most glorious époque in the annals of Spain', as Prescott famously called the reign of Ferdinand and Isabella – so, imperceptibly at first, it laid the foundations of its own demise:

> The modern Spaniard who surveys these vestiges of a giant race, the tokens of his nation's degeneracy, must turn for relief to the prouder and earlier period of her history, when only such works could have been achieved; and it is no wonder that he should be led, in his

enthusiasm, to invest it with a romantic and exaggerated colouring. Such a period in Spain cannot be looked for in the eighteenth, still less in the seventeenth century, for the nation had then reached the lowest ebb of his fortunes; nor in the close of the sixteenth, for the desponding language of the Cortes shows the work of decay and depopulation had then already begun. It can only be found in the first half of the century, in the reign of Ferdinand and Isabella, and that of their successor, Charles the Fifth; in which last, the state, was carried onward in the career of prosperity, in spite of the ignorance and mismanagement of those who guided it [...] Thus it is that the seed sown under a good system continues to yield fruit under a bad one.[31]

In formulating his overall hypothesis, Prescott set the trajectories of America and Spain alongside one another, the former representing 'the new' and the latter 'the old'. Habsburg Spain was seen as a nation separated from the European (i.e. Protestant) mainstream and bereft of the progress and prosperity that flowed from its wake. His seminal idea or 'paradigm' – the antithesis between Spanish decadence and American progress that he conceptualized – responded to nationalist sensitivities and had a considerable impact on the outlook of his contemporaries, including the way Spaniards themselves constructed their own image of the past. His writing continued to exert a major influence on succeeding generations of historians on both sides of the Atlantic until the mid-twentieth century, though his celebration of American achievements and potential gave it a special significance in the United States.

The work of fellow American scholar Henry Charles Lea (1825–1909), a publisher who wrote history in his spare time, complements that of Prescott. In 1898 (the year of the Spanish–American War that simultaneously ended Spain's imperial era while initiating that of the United States) Lea wrote an essay on 'The Decadence of Spain', published in the *Atlantic Monthly*, in which he identified three root causes of Spanish decadence: (a) pride, which led to the disdain of honest labour; (b) conservatism, which resulted in the rejection of all innovation; and (c) clericalism, from which developed the ferocious spirit of intolerance embodied in the Inquisition:

This unreasoning religious ardour culminated in the Inquisition, established for the purpose of securing the supreme good of unblemished purity and uniformity of belief. ... The real significance of the Inquisition lay in the isolation to which it condemned the land, and its benumbing influence on the intellectual development of the people. ... While the rest of the civilised world was bounding forward in a career of progress ... invention and discovery were unknown at home, and their admission from abroad was regarded with jealousy. Recuperative power was thus wholly lacking to offset the destructive effects of misgovernment, the national conservatism was intensified, and a habit of mind was engendered which has kept Spain to this day a virtual survival of the Renaissance.[32]

Like Prescott, Lea also attacked the Habsburg absolutism that prevented the nation from developing the liberal institutions necessary to lead it into the modern world and subjected everything to the will of the monarch. 'In many respects', he remarked, looking down on them from his own America's high peak, 'the Spaniard is still living in the sixteenth century, unable to assimilate the ideas of the nineteenth, or to realize that his country is no longer the mistress of the sea and the dominating power of the land'.[33] Lea's theories echo with a resonance typical of the liberal philosophy that he espoused, tinged with Black Legend rhetoric. But the subsequent research he undertook on the history of the Spanish Inquisition was marked by a significant change in his approach.

Lea had already written a critical study of the medieval Inquisition (*History of the Inquisition of the Middle Ages*) in the late 1880s and now turned his attention to the Spanish Inquisition, driven partly by his interest in the institution's profound impact on the fortunes of the nation, but also by the major research opportunities such a study offered in the late nineteenth century. His four-volume *A History of the Inquisition of Spain* (1906–7) was written in a style considerably more objective and measured in its analysis than his previous works, in accordance with emerging trends in the writing and foundation of history, and is still regarded today as the most extensive and scholarly work on the Inquisition. Lea had begun to read literature in the field in the 1860s, including Puigblanch and Llorente, and managed to avail himself of books, materials and documents from all over Europe through contacts and correspondence. He felt that other scholars (including Ranke) had only skimmed the surface of its history and that Catholic writers had too much of a vested interest to get to the root of the matter. In 1895 he made contact with the national archive at Simancas, where the records of the Inquisition had recently been deposited. Lea was fortunate to be among the first international scholars to undertake original research, in his case conducted via private assistants employed on his behalf, into the vast inquisitorial records, just as the archive was being classified and reorganized.[34] The extensive use of sources and application of critical method by Lea and fellow scholars radically transformed the historical discourse, turning the late nineteenth and early twentieth centuries into 'the golden age of historiography on the Inquisition'.[35]

Lea's work on the Spanish Inquisition – in which he sought to explain the circumstances surrounding the assumption and subsequent dismantling of its power within society – brought him to understand that the inquisitors and their victims were prisoners of time and that the modern historian had to be cautious about the way in which he made moral judgements about the past. Lea accepted that the Inquisition was established for reasons which Spanish monarchs saw as being legitimate in the context of their rule:

> Isabella and her Habsburg descendants were but obeying the dictates of conscience and executing the laws of the Church, when they sought to suppress heresy and apostasy by force, and they might well deem it both duty and good policy at a time when it was universally taught that unity of faith was the surest guarantee of the happiness and prosperity of nations.[36]

He argued that the Inquisition, 'while enforcing conformity as to dogma and outward observance, failed to inspire genuine respect for religion'[37] and thus did not fulfil its prime purpose. Instead it became the official instrument of intolerance that besmirched the Spanish character and paralysed the intellectual development of Spain for generations. While he acknowledged the severity of its practices, he stood out from previous scholars in pointing to the unreliability of the statistical evidence surrounding the number of those persecuted and the methods employed to extract confessions that he felt had been exaggerated in the popular imagination (and for which he held Llorente and other polemical writers partly responsible, on account of their fallacious guesswork). He maintained that it was less cruel than secular tribunals and that it had a more favourable reputation than the Roman Inquisition, thus setting the agenda for the revisionist history of its practices that would follow in the later twentieth century.[38] In his conclusion, and in accordance with the liberal, empirical approach to historical discourse that he espoused in this study, he sought to draw a balance between the evil nature of the institution and the zeal for the faith that underpinned it, that is, between its method and the mentality of the age:

> The Church had taught for centuries that implicit acceptance of its dogmas and blind obedience to its commands were the only avenues to salvation; that heresy was treason to God, its extermination the highest service to God and the highest duty to man. This became a universal belief ... In Spain, on account of its peculiar circumstances, this resolve to enforce unity of belief, in the conviction that it was essential to human happiness here and hereafter, led to the framing of a system of so-called justice more iniquitous than has been evolved by the cruellest despotism. ... The great lesson taught by the history of the Inquisition is that the attempt of man to control the conscience of his fellows reacts upon himself; he may inflict misery, but, in due time, that misery recoils on him or on his descendants and the full penalty is exacted with interest. Never has the attempt been made so thoroughly, so continuously or with such means of success as in Spain, and never has the consequent retribution been so palpable and so severe.[39]

Lea's work, through its use of original materials and critical techniques, set new standards in inquisitorial scholarship, resurrecting it and the decline theories it generated from the traditional 'black' versus 'white' interpretations that had characterized Spanish historiography since the sixteenth century.

The nineteenth century marked a new phase in the historiography of Spain's decline, when professional standards in the writing of history began to impact on scholarship. Although the political and ideological divide between liberal and conservative Spanish historians continued to be in evidence, by the end of the century they were beginning to converge in their judgements, for example in their acknowledgement of the repressive role of the Inquisition, the negative effects of empire and failings of monarchy. A notably more measured, self-critical approach to the whole decline phenomenon began to emerge from within the conservative school, as observed through the work of Cánovas del Castillo. At the same time, foreign scholars such as Lea tempered their liberal analysis of the root causes of decadence with an appreciation of the difficulties Spain faced in acknowledging the errors of the past, accepting the need for change and entering the modern era. The events of 1898 accelerated that process of self-reflection.

Notes

1 Cited by Leonard Krieger, *Ranke. The Meaning of History* (Chicago, IL and London, 1977) p. 5.
2 Richard Herr, 'The Constitution of 1812 and the Spanish road to Parliamentary Monarchy', in Isser Woloch (ed.), *Revolution and the Meaning of Freedom in the Nineteenth Century* (Stanford, CA, 1996), pp. 65–102.
3 Juan Antonio Llorente, *Historia Crítica de la Inquisición Española*, 4 vols (Madrid, 1980), I, pp. 1–3.
4 See Stephen Haliczer, 'Inquisition myth and inquisition history: the abolition of the Holy Office and the development of Spanish political ideology', in Angel Alcalá (ed.), *The Spanish Inquisition and the Inquisitorial Mind* (Boulder, CO, 1987), pp. 524–6.
5 Llorente, *Historia Crítica*, I, p. 8.
6 Ibid., pp. 5–6.
7 Ibid., p. 7.
8 Cited by Robert Hughes, *Goya* (London, 2004), p. 164.
9 Francisco Bethencourt, *The Inquisition. A Global History, 1478–1834* (Cambridge, 2009), pp. 10–13.
10 On Modesto Lafuente, see George L. Vásquez, 'The historians of nineteenth-century Spain' (PhD thesis, Columbia University, 1978), pp. 71–2, 79–81, 91–8, 117–18 and Gonzalo Pasamar, *Apologia and Criticism. Historical Writing in Spain 1500–2000* (Bern, 2010), pp. 62–89.
11 Cited by Vásquez, 'Historians of ninteenth-century Spain', pp. 105–6.
12 Vásquez, 'Historians', pp. 257–79; J. Lynch, 'Menéndez Pelayo as a historian', *Bulletin of Hispanic Studies*, 33: 4 (1956), 187–201.
13 Cited by Vásquez, 'Historians', p. 282.
14 Carolyn P. Boyd, *Historia Patria. Politics, History and National Identity in Spain, 1875–1975* (Princeton, NJ, 1997), pp. 68–72.
15 Haliczer, 'Inquisition myth', pp. 530–4.
16 Douglas W. Foard, 'The Spanish Fichte: Menéndez y Pelayo', *Journal of Contemporary History*, 14:1 (1979), 94–6.
17 Boyd, *Historia Patria*, p. 243.
18 Cited by Lynch, 'Menéndez Pelayo as a historian', 191.

19 Cited by Vásquez, 'Historians', p. 289.
20 On Cánovas del Castillo, see George L. Vásquez, 'Cánovas and the decline of Spain', *Mediterranean Historical Review*, 7:1 (1992), 66–91.
21 Cited in ibid., 73.
22 Ibid., 74.
23 Ibid., 75.
24 Ibid., 76.
25 Ibid., 78.
26 Cited by Vásquez, 'Historians', p. 184.
27 J.L. Motley, *History of the United Netherlands*, 4 vols (London, 1860–67), Vol. III, pp. 517, 534.
28 Richard L. Kagan, 'Prescott's paradigm: American historical scholarship and the decline of Spain', *The American Historical Review*, 101:2 (April, 1996), 423–46.
29 William H. Prescott, *History of the Reign of Philip II, King of Spain*, 3 vols (Philadelphia, PA, 1882), Vol. I, p. 133.
30 Ibid., pp. 408–9.
31 William H. Prescott, *History of the Reign of Ferdinand and Isabella, the Catholic*, 3 vols (Boston, MA, 1844), Vol. 3, pp. 462–3 and 495.
32 H.C. Lea, 'The decadence of Spain', *Atlantic Monthly*, 82 (1898), 40.
33 Lea, 'The decadence of Spain', 40–1.
34 Gustav Henningsen, 'The archives and historiography of the Spanish Inquisition', in Gustav Henningsen and John Tedeschi (eds), *The Inquisition in Early Modern Europe. Studies in Sources and Methods* (Delkab, IL, 1986), pp. 61–4.
35 Edward Peters, *Inquisition* (Berkeley ans Los Angeles, CA), 1988, pp. 287–93.
36 H.C. Lea, *A History of the Inquisition of Spain*, 4 vols (London, 1906–7), Vol. IV, pp. 505–6.
37 Ibid., p. 504.
38 Ibid., Vol. II, pp. 2–3.
39 Ibid., Vol. IV, pp. 531–3.

5

The early twentieth century: imperialism and decline

The advance of the Spanish Empire was certain to be arrested, and the stately process of territorial aggrandizement, which had gone on virtually unchecked since the beginning of the Reconquest, to be succeeded by disintegration and decline. (R.B. Merriman, The *Rise of the Spanish Empire in the Old World and the New* [New York, 1934], Vol. IV, p. 402)

In 1898, following a short, three-year period of confrontation, Spain lost its struggle with the United States to retain possession over the last of its overseas colonies. By the Treaty of Paris of 28 November 1898, it renounced its possession of Cuba, Puerto Rico and the Philippines, marking the end of four hundred years of discovery, colonization and empire building under its rule. Although the majority of Spanish American colonies had gained their independence at the beginning of the century, 1898 marked the final defeat. The editorial in the daily Spanish newspaper *El Liberal* demonstrates how the left-wing Spanish press reacted to the event:

An ill-fated day

Today the Treaty of Paris will be signed, by which Spain renounces its possession of Cuba, Puerto Rico and the Philippines. Today will see a definitive end to the golden legacy, initiated by Christopher Columbus in 1492 and by Ferdinand Magellan in 1521. ... Today we are no longer a colonial power, nor do we possess any of the pride and status associated with second or third rate powers. Holland, Denmark and Portugal own and exploit vast amounts of land in Asia, Africa and Oceania. We have lost everything. All we have left are a few inhospitable tiny islands in the gulf of Guinea, a few inches of the north Moroccan coast and half a dozen or so crags bearing the sinister name of outposts. After 400 years we are returning from the West Indies, which we discovered, from the Far East, which we civilized, as tenants who have been evicted, as intruders who have been expelled, as children who have been incapacitated, as unruly people who must be shut away. From now on our national symbol will no longer be a lion poised between ownership of two hemispheres. It will be one of those unfortunate men who have come back from our colonies, without arms or blood, merely hanging onto life. Men like this now represent Spain, consumed by anaemia, exhausted by starvation rather than by defeat, and as much devoid of energy as resources.[1]

The dramatic watershed of 1898 was accompanied by a profound sense of national disaster. The crisis prompted a group of Spanish historians, intellectuals and philosophers, collectively known as the Generation of '98, to reflect upon the causes of Spain's failure as nation, of which the loss of empire and status as a colonial power was seen as the culmination, and seek the means for its regeneration, in much the same way as the *arbitristas* had sought to reverse the symptoms of decline at the beginning of the seventeenth century. A prolonged process of introspection began. Members of the movement were broadly divided into two opposite bands: the modernizers (referred to as *europeístas*), who attributed Spain's misfortunes to its isolation from Europe, and the traditionalists (known as *casticistas*), who advocated recovery through a reassertion of conventional Spanish values. They represented a continuation of the old struggle between liberals and conservatives that had characterized Spanish historiography in the previous century and the emerging left- and right-wing political thinkers of their own generation. For the former (including Joaquín Costa and José Ortega y Gasset), the key to Spain's progress in the aftermath of 1898 lay in leaving behind her imperial ambitions, recovering her strength of leadership and opening herself up intellectually to Europe and beyond. For the latter (including José Martínez Ruiz and Ramiro de Maeztu), Spain should take pride in her imperial achievements, particularly her heritage in Spanish America, and seek to rebuild the crusading spirit that gave rise to its greatness as a nation in past centuries. Meanwhile, professional historians such as Rafael Altamira and Ramón Menéndez Pidal sought to steer a more balanced course in their contributions to the historical discourse, despite their own progressive credentials. At the same time, foreign scholars such as the American Roger Bigelow Merriman took the opportunity to reassess Spain's predicament through the lens of its imperial misfortunes, the latter providing a sharp contrast with America's own predominance on the world stage – a phenomenon already highlighted by his fellow countrymen Prescott and Lea.

The work of members of the Generation of '98 serves to illustrate the divergent points of view on 'the problem of Spain' that emerged in the opening decades of the twentieth century and the differing stands it would take in the conflict between modernization and tradition. As well as examining the causes of the so-called 'Disaster' of 1898, they explored Spain's general backwardness as a power and its decline from former greatness. Spanish writers and intellectuals also approached the crisis from philosophical perspectives, seeking to identify the essential flaws in the Spanish character and concept of national identity that gave rise to its degeneration. Far from being anti-Spanish, the men of '98 were driven by an intense sense of patriotism, and a desire to seek in Spain's past, its culture and its people solutions to its present predicament.

In 1896, the scholar and diplomat Ángel Ganivet (1865–98) published his *Ideárium Español* [*Interpretation of Spain*], written on the eve of the collapse of Spanish power in Central America, in which he expounded a philosophy on the condition and future direction of Spain that essentially took a middle course. In examining Spain's relationship with its colonial past, Ganivet accepted the conquest of the New World as intrinsic to its Catholic mission, but proposed that Spain's attempted political dominance of Europe was a fundamental mistake, since it diverted the peninsula from its path of independence and instigated a foreign policy commitment that led to the nation's protracted decline, from which it was yet to fully recover. Now, he advocated, it must renounce the model of greatness as measured in terms of territorial and economic power and concentrate its energies instead on affirming the primacy of the ideals and spirit of Spanish civilization, which no other nation could rival. If Spain had gone astray by pursuing an imperial agenda, then the solution was to decentralize and rebuild the community, the municipality and the region to work in harmony with one another. Spain had over-reached itself and now needed a period of introspection and consolidation before embarking on a new destiny:[2]

> The exploration and conquest of America, which opened such a breach in our national life, had also its justification in our character, in our faith, in the providential destiny which fell so heavily on our shoulders. But our action in the centre of Europe was a policy of immeasurable absurdity, an illogicality whose only excuse was and is the fact that it was based on ideas then in vogue in the matter of political theory and practice. When Spain, a peninsular nation, set about acting like the continental nations, she condemned herself to certain ruin. Whereas a country is strengthened by acquiring new territories within its natural sphere of action, it is, on the other hand, weakened by the absorption of those which involve contingencies opposed to its special permanent interest. ... A wrong road in policy destroys a nation, be it the greatest nation in the world. Spain committed this mistake. [...] A regeneration of the whole life of Spain can have no starting point other than the concentration of all our energies within our own territory. We must fasten with lock, chain and bolt every door by which the Spanish spirit escaped from Spain and spread itself over the four points of the compass, whence salvation is looked for even to-day. [...] Spain was the first European nation to be aggrandized by a policy of expansion and conquest; it was the first to decay and to bring to an end the material stage of her evolution; it must now be the first to work towards a political and social restoration of an entirely new order. [...] The origin of our decadence and our actual prostration is to be found in our excessive action, our involvement in enterprises disproportionate to our power.[3]

A year earlier, in 1895, the writer and young professor of classics at Salamanca University, Miguel de Unamuno (1864–1936), published his *En torno al casticismo* [*On the essence of Spain*], in which he expressed a contrary view to that championed by fellow intellectual Ganivet. For Unamuno, Spain reached the height of its power when its borders were open to Europe and fell into decline when barriers to expansionism were erected and the exclusive spirit of Castilian *casticismo* stifled the character and vitality of the *pueblo*. He believed that Spain needed to rediscover its traditional 'intra-historical' roots (referred to as *la tradición eterna*), common to all humanity. National regeneration from the aridity and stagnation of contemporary life was dependent on Spain allowing the infiltration of invigorating currents of modernity and progress from abroad:

> Castile was great when it opened itself up fully to outside influences and spread itself around the world; then, it shut itself off and has not surfaced since. [...] The spiritual misery of Spain derives from the policy of isolation borne of inquisitorial protectionism that smothered the Reformation at birth and prevented Spain from embracing Europe [...]; only by opening ourselves up to Europe, absorbing continental influences, trusting that we will not lose our personality by doing so ... will we regenerate this moral fibre.[4]

Unamuno, therefore, argued that Spain's position at the crossroads of Europe, Africa, the Mediterranean and the New World, offered a basis for urging not a policy of independence or isolationism, as proposed by Ganivet, but one of open frontiers and closer contact with other cultures, leading to the revitalization of the spirit of the nation.[5] 'Spain is still to be discovered, and only Europeanized Spaniards will discover it,'[6] he wrote. But in the aftermath of 1898, Unamuno became disillusioned with both the political leadership of Spain and the European ideal. Having championed the Europeanization of Spain in the mid-1890s, he adapted his position to become an advocate of the Hispanization of Europe, upholding his belief in the Spanish people to shake off their restrictive past and share their common tradition with their European partners.

Joaquín Costa (1846–1911), the son of an Aragonese peasant and a self-educated lawyer and writer, was a firm advocate of Spain's Europeanization and the prophet of *regeneración* [regenerationism]. He expounded these ideas in his *Reconstitución y europeización de España* [*Reconstitution and Europeanization of Spain*] of 1924, a post-1898 reflection on the historical roots of Spain's backwardness. Costa deplored Spain's isolation from the mainstream of European political and cultural thought. He called for the destruction of *caciquismo* [political clientelism, linked to electoral corruption], which prevailed in nineteenth-century

Spanish politics, and the urgent modernization of the country's social, political and economic structures. An enormous effort was required for Spain to incorporate itself into Europe and match its progress after four centuries of resistance, but only in that way could it advance as a nation. Costa coined the dictum 'School, larder and double-lock the tomb of El Cid', to summarise the policy by which the Europeanization of Spain was to be achieved: by a radical reform of education and by concentrating efforts on making the country more economically productive, particularly in the agricultural sector. To begin with, he recommended, all the heroic names and feats of Spain's past, such as those of the Christian warrior El Cid, should be permanently wiped off the slate, religious education under the auspices of the Catholic Church be abandoned, and young people be encouraged to reconstruct their nation's prosperity. Relinquishing all thoughts of past grandeur, especially overseas adventure, Spaniards needed to dedicate themselves to the serious business of rebuilding peninsular Spain. He was of the opinion that the regeneration of Spain could only be achieved by means of revolution. In his *Oligarquía y Caciquismo* [*Oligarchy and Despotism*] (1901), he called for a fundamental renewal of the current system of Spanish government in accordance with the European model, to ensure its future as a nation. A progressive Spain needed to be created: one that was wealthy, free, strong and open to outside influences. It was necessary for what he called the 'live forces' of society 'to spontaneously found a new Spain in the peninsula: that is a Spain that is rich and able to eat; a Spain that is cultured and able to think; a Spain that is free and can govern; a Spain that is strong and can conquer; in short a Spain at one with humanity, that when you cross its boundaries does not feel alien or as if it belongs to another planet or century'.[7] Costa's condemnation of Spanish tradition and culture, including its colonial past, typical among radical intellectuals in early twentieth-century Spain, was coupled with a mounting sense of disillusion and despair, hence his unrestrained advocacy of change by force.

The republican philosopher José Ortega y Gasset (1888–1955) was one of the foremost members of the modernizing wing of the Generation of '98 in the early part of the twentieth century. Unlike many of his contemporaries, he did not see Spain's problems as deriving exclusively from its failure to embrace the modern European model. His plan for the regeneration of Spain required it to draw closer to Europe, but while still steering its own distinctive destiny. In his *España Invertebrada* (*Invertebrate Spain*) of 1922, he argued that Spain's crisis was one principally derived from its historical development as a nation, forged by Castile. In the sixteenth century, working in conjunction with the monarchy and the Church, it invested all its energies into uniting Spain and raising it to greatness through imperial conquest. That enterprise culminated in the colonization of the New World, 'the only truly great thing which Spain has done'.[8] He attributed its success to the efforts of the Spanish people: 'The Spanish colonization of America was the work of the common people ... it was the *pueblo*, the common people themselves, who, without conscious design, without directors, without deliberate tactics, engendered other peoples.'[9] However, in the absence of an effective leadership (a 'backbone') to provide discipline and instruction from above – and which had hampered Spain's development as a nation since – they had not been able to take the venture forward.[10] He contended that, from the end of the sixteenth century onwards, Spain's history had been characterized by its decadence: 'Then we see that everything which has happened in Spain from the year 1580 up to the present time is disintegration and decay.'[11] He linked the process to the gradual collapse of Spain's empire, beginning in the Low Countries, until the loss of its final colonies in the Americas and Far East in 1898, and to the progressive disintegration of Spain itself from the periphery to the centre. He saw the rise of harmful 'particularist' tendencies in peripheral regions such as Catalonia and the Basque Provinces, and subsequently affecting all sectors of society, as being a consequence of the collapse of the central, cohesive role forged by Castile. In the seventeenth century, in contrast to the sixteenth, it lost its drive, inspiration and selflessness, resulting in a reversal of the nation's fortunes. The empire makers became its breakers:

> Castile made Spain, and Castile has unmade it. As the initial nucleus in Iberian amalgamation, Castile managed to overcome its own particularism and invited the other peninsular peoples to collaborate in a tremendous plan for life in common. Castile invented great and inspiring enterprises, placed herself at the service of high moral,

religious and judicious ideals, drew up a plan for the social order, set it forth as a norm that the better man would be preferred to the worse, the active to the lazy, the clever to the stupid, the noble to the vile. All these aspirations, norms, habits, ideals, were kept alive and active for a long time. Men drew inspiration from them, lived according to their light, believed in them, respected them and feared them. But as soon as we come in sight of the Spain of Philip III we note a terrible transformation. At first glance nothing seems changed, but on closer inspection everything proves to have turned into papier maché. Whatever we touch sounds hollow. The fiery words of former days go on being repeated, but they strike no echo in the heart; the inspiring ideals have become mere topics of conversation. No one starts anything new, either in politics, or science, or the realm of morals. All the activity that is left is spent 'in *not* making anything new', in conserving the past – institution and dogma alike – in smothering all initiative, all ferment of innovation. Castile has become its own opposite – suspicious, narrow, sordid, bitter. It is no longer occupied in giving force to the life of other regions. Jealous of them, it abandons them to their own resources and takes no further interest in anything that happens to them.[12]

The *casticista* and anti-Europeanist, José Martínez Ruiz (1876–1967), better known by his literary pseudonym of Azorín, in his inaugural speech to the Spanish Royal Academy of 1924 (and later expounded in his *La Hora de España* [*An Hour of Spain*] [1930]), maintained that the idea of Spanish decadence had been viewed through a distorted lens by historians (notably French and English), being considered only in relation to the mother country rather than to its possessions in the American continent. Although the diminution of Spanish power in Europe was indisputable in the second half of the seventeenth century, he regarded the success of its enterprise in the New World as having been fundamentally neglected as a parallel phenomenon:

> The idea of decadence is old in Spain. Spaniards and foreigners alike have spoken at length, for some time now, of Spain's decline. Let us react against this idea. ... Decadence has not existed. A world has just been discovered. Twenty nations are created. A single language blots out a multitude of indigenous languages. Vast works of irrigation are constructed. Roads are laid out. Forests are cleared and land is broken and tilled. Extremely high mountains are scaled, and immensely broad rivers sailed upon. Vast throngs are instructed and

trained. Identical municipal institutions are spread over thousands of towns and cities. In short, industry, trade, navigation, agriculture, herding, arise on a new piece of planet, and enrich peoples and nations. And who has carried out this gigantic piece of work? All the nations of Europe together? ... No; a single nation, alone, with the help of no one: Spain. ... Let us not limit our view to the area of Spain. Spain is the Peninsula and the twenty American countries. Spain, with the discovery and colonization of America, created a branch of herself that had to be greater than the mother house. ... The idea of decadence will gradually disappear in the measure in which the spiritual space that exists between Spain and America also disappears.[13]

Indeed, following the events of 1898 and the annexation of the last disparate elements of what had once been the Spanish Empire, a change of heart took place among many of the Hispanic nations. They became aware of the threat to their independence posed by American and Soviet imperialism and looked to renew their historic cultural links with Spain. From this grew the celebration of the *Día de la Raza* (1919), later renamed as *Día de la Hispanidad* (1957), on 12 October (the date when Columbus first set foot in the New World) to commemorate Spain's imperial achievements and its racial and cultural contribution to western civilization. The principal defender of this patriotic cause was the political theorist and journalist Ramiro de Maeztu (1875–1936), who, in his book *Defensa de la Hispanidad* [*Defence of Spanishness*] of 1934, claimed 'Spanishness', based on the notion of spiritual 'universalism', to be the key concept upon which the confederation of Hispanic nations was founded and which would ensure its unity and strength in the future. The recapturing of that tradition represented the means by which Spain could once again aspire towards greatness:

By discovering the maritime routes of East and West, Spain completed the physical unity of the world; by securing the triumph, at Trent, of the dogma that secures to all men the possibility of salvation, and therefore of progress, Spain brought into being the necessary standard that enables us to speak of the moral unity of the human race. Consequently, Spanishness created universal history, and nothing else in the world, apart from Christianity, can be compared to what it achieved. ... Thus we perceive the spirit of

Spanishness as a light from on high. ... Rather than being linked by race or by geography, our community is united by the spirit. It is in the spirit ... where we find the history [of Catholicism] that makes us who we are.[14]

Ramiro de Maeztu's promotion of 'Spanishness', by emphasizing the patriotic ideals that had contributed to the success of the Christian Reconquest and its Catholic mission overseas – a commitment to militant, crusading Catholicism – and by calling for a return to those historic principles in the present, provided an expedient rallying call for the authoritarian right wing in early twentieth-century Spain, which pursued its cause in the Spanish Civil War in the spirit of a religious crusade.[15]

One of the most influential professional historians to emerge from the Generation of '98 was Rafael Altamira y Crevea (1866–1951).[16] Altamira, who had a multifaceted career as a judge, journalist and politician before becoming a teacher and professor, was deeply affected by the wave of pessimism that engulfed his country at the turn of the century but believed that Spain needed to counteract the psychology of failure. His hope for a reversal of this trend lay with Spaniards themselves, but their lack of educational opportunity meant they were unaware of their potential to unleash change. He believed that knowledge of national history was crucial to this process and a requisite for the advancement of modern civilization. Along with fellow modernizers such as Joaquín Costa, he deplored the failure of historical studies in Spain to keep pace with trends in European historiography and vigorously promoted the raising of standards of scholarship and its wide dissemination, beginning at school level. The two principal functions of the historian were, in his view, to advance the writing of objective history and to increase its accessibility to the ordinary Spaniard, who either remained ignorant of his own nation's past or was in possession of a distorted version of it. He felt that historians had an key role to play in restoring Spain's national reputation, tarnished by the Black Legend and the preponderance of the theme of decadence, by contesting the myths of history and challenging the negative characteristics attributed to Spaniards since time immemorial. Altamira actively sought to promote cultural exchange and solidarity with Spanish America in order to suppress the old prejudices relating to the colonial enterprise. In his role as professor at the University of Oviedo, where he had established a university extension programme, he undertook a successful lecture tour of Latin American countries in 1909–10 to bring education to the people. He sought in his writing to present a more balanced view of Spanish history by drawing attention to Spaniards' positive contribution, such as their 'civilization' of the American continent, and thus to enable them to engage more objectively and critically with their own past and present. In 1898 he advocated that one of the essential conditions for national regeneration was to 'restore the credit of our history, with the goal of returning to the Spanish people their faith in their native qualities and aptitude for civilized life, and of taking advantage of the useful elements that the knowledge and conduct of past times offer us'.[17]

Given his vision of the function of history, Altamira wrote for wide audiences. His four-volume *Historia de España y de la civilización española* [*History of Spanish Civilization*] (1899–1911) is generally considered to be his most important contribution to the general history of Spain, covering the period from earliest civilization to the Napoleonic wars, that would set the standard for the next generation of Spanish scholars. His work transcended mere political history, focusing on subjects previously ignored by Spanish historians, such as industrial development, the judicial system, social and economic structures as well as the nation's cultural achievements. He deliberately adopted a non-partisan line in his assessment of those controversial events and phenomena in Spanish history that aroused most passion, including the impact of the Inquisition and the expulsion of religious minorities. His aim was to record the results of modern research without prejudice and allow his readers to formulate their own judgements.

In his evaluation of the phenomenon of decline, Altamira highlighted Spain's efforts to secure and maintain hegemony in Europe as constituting the primary cause of its dramatic reversal of fortune in the seventeenth century. Essentially, he argued, Spain was unrealistic in its aims and inept in carrying them through. Its human and material resources were insufficient to support the imperial policies of Charles V and the religious wars of Philip II, draining Castile in particular of its manpower and wealth and resulting in the neglect of the nation's own internal needs. He characterized the two sixteenth-century monarchs not as tyrants scheming ruthlessly to humble foreign adversaries but, rather, as tragic figures trapped in their own impossible dreams. Each 'tried to realise in full the ideals of the nation and the Empire', yet 'the demands made upon them were too much for human strength ... and it is not surprising that both broke down before them'.[18] As well as underlining the inevitable failure of its imperialist ventures, Altamira also pointed to the contributions made by Spaniards to European civilization, in particular via their formulation of a legal system [*el derecho indiano*] that was used to govern the natives in the New World. Far from being a relentless exploiter and profiteer, he argued, the Spanish government sought to promote social and civil equality between colonizers and indigenous peoples, constituting a revolutionary departure from the European pattern of colonization. 'The principal of freedom in the eyes of the law', he noted, 'formed the basis of a legal ruling, which had no precedent in the history of colonization and no contemporary imitators.'[19] He thus sought to overturn the stereotypical notion of the Spaniard as the oppressive colonial power subjecting a weaker, inferior race to its will, as expounded by Las Casas, promoting instead its championing of concepts of equality in international law and thus injecting balance into the debate. Although he did not create a distinct school of history or specialize in the early modern period, Altamira nevertheless stands out as a historian in this field for his contribution to the reappraisal of decline as a phenomenon that was foreseeable and one that all great civilizations experienced as a natural part of their development, as well as for his pedagogical vision of history.

Ramón Menéndez Pidal (1868–1969), who held the chair in Romance Philology at the University of Madrid for most of his career, figures alongside Altamira as one of the most distinguished professional historians and philologists to make a major contribution to the advancement of Spanish historiography in the opening decades of the twentieth century. Menéndez Pidal, a former student of Menéndez y Pelayo, was committed to the importance of undertaking meticulous original research in keeping with modern methods of historical enquiry. In common with Altamira, he considered the raising of standards of scholarship to be fundamental for Spaniards to gain a more accurate and profound appreciation of their own history and to take pride in their national achievements, thereby counteracting the disillusion characteristic of the post-1898 generation. Of particular interest to him was Spain's imperial tradition and commitment to collective enterprise, the importance of which he traced back to medieval times and whose triumph was epitomized in the heroic figure of El Cid. He sought to rehabilitate the Castilian warrior as the embodiment of a national ideal of political and cultural unity born out of the Christian Reconquest that could once again inspire the people. In a provocative essay, *Los Españoles en su historia* [*The Spaniards in their History*] (1950), he examined the whole panorama of Spanish history to show how modern tendencies were shaped by their past. He saw one of the peaks of Spain's historical development being reached in the medieval period, when it assimilated eastern and western cultures and accomplished its destiny, 'which was to serve as a link between the two heterogeneous worlds of Christianity and Islam'.[20] For Menéndez Pidal, the founding of the Spanish empire overseas did not constitute a severe reversal in its development, as some members of his generation suggested, but a remarkable step forward for mankind. 'At the very moment when the ancient notion of European-history laden Empire was dying out', he observed, 'there arose the Spanish empire, without history, the first one of modern times not anchored to Roman and medieval law, but eager to discover new standards of natural and international law.'[21] He felt that Spain's achievement in the New World, notably its spiritual accomplishment and desire to establish the legitimacy of its rule, had been over-shadowed by the emphasis placed on the injustices and atrocities committed and, in common with Altamira, held Las Casas partly responsible on account of his fictitious, defamatory testimony. In similar vein to Ortega y Gasset, he attributed the decline of empire to the failure to select and recruit men of merit and ability to take forward its ventures and to the loss of a sense of national purpose that had characterized its greatest historical moments. To make his point, he cited a seventeenth-century observer who noted that 'Empires were successful as long as they went in search of men and brought them in from the deserts to govern. If this were the method used in Spain there would be no lack of men to fill the posts nor would so many be forgotten.'[22] He perceived the regional revolts that took place in Portugal and Catalonia in 1640 as being prompted by the inhabitants' unwillingness to contribute to the imperial enterprise, and attributed the dismantling of the political unity of Spain that followed to 'the disappearance of the spirit and the ancient virtue which had created empire'.[23] Although Menéndez Pidal's thesis differed in varying degrees from that of other intellectuals of the time (he was both a Europeanizer and an admirer of Spain's Muslim past), he shared in the collective aim of fellow historians to remove political dissensions and ideological persuasions from the debate over Spain's decline and in their belief in the nation's regenerative possibilities: 'If Spaniards can join together for the great collective tasks before them, if they can agree in establishing an era based on justice and selectivity free from party prejudice, they will at last bring to an end these tossings of the ship of State and set her on a steady course towards the high destinies of the nation.'[24]

At the beginning of the twentieth century interest in the early modern period on the part of foreign scholars was revived, following Spain's relinquishing of the remnants of its once vast overseas empire in 1898, inviting a reconsideration of the circumstances surrounding its imperial 'rise' and 'fall'. British and American historians – themselves the protagonists of empire – took a particular interest in the theme. Their reading of the evidence at their disposal varied according to their approach to historical studies as being either events based or problem based, and their ability to separate their own partisanship from their discourse.

The Liberal Party supporter and independent scholar, Martin A.S. Hume (1843–1910), became a dedicated writer on Spain's early modern fortunes and rescued the field from neglect for a British readership. Hume was inspired by his family's close connections with Bourbon Spain: his maternal ancestor, Andrew Hume, had been recruited as a foreign entrepreneur by the government of Charles III and in 1788 became director of the royal button factory in Madrid. He regularly visited his relatives in the capital as a young man, where he observed the troubled political landscape of the 1860s at first hand. In 1892, having discovered his vocation in history, Hume succeeded Pascual de Gayangos as editor of the Calendar of State Papers, publishing eight volumes of state correspondence between England and Spain for the period 1545–1603. He also made contributions to the study of Spain's decline to the first edition of *The Cambridge Modern History*, published in 1906. Hume was one of the first British historians to make use of printed sources in Spanish, including contemporary accounts and collections of original documents, as well as diplomatic correspondence and manuscript records held in the British Museum. For all his natural sympathy with the Spanish people and the empirical foundations of his narrative, Hume's account of Spain's seventeenth-century decline and the part played in it by empire was essentially that of a late-Victorian Englishman of Protestant persuasion, with an overtly liberal take on events.

In his *The Spanish People* (1901), Hume condemned the excessive zeal and fanaticism that underpinned Spaniards' imperialist ambitions and that led them to believe, erroneously, in their own superiority and invincibility as a nation. In the first half of the sixteenth century, he contended, Spaniards were 'intoxicated with the grandeur of the mission confided to them, as they thought, by the Almighty to suppress heresy throughout the world' and 'welcomed blindly the erection of the Inquisition into a political instrument because it gave sanction to the idea that they were better than other people'.[25] In relation to the decision taken by Olivares at the beginning of the reign of Philip IV that Spain should re-engage on the battlefields of Europe in the Thirty Years' War (1618–48) and rekindle its imperial mantle in the name of Catholicism, Hume regarded this action as upholding the arrogant claim that a desolate, ruined Castile could dictate to the whole world the faith it should obey. Such a policy, he claimed in his *Cambridge Modern History* essay (1934), epitomized 'the obstinate clinging to the old boastful tradition of Spain's right and power to interfere in the religious affairs of other countries, and to play a predominant role in European politics'.[26] It was this, according to Hume, that lay at the heart of Spain's decline as an imperial nation, killing off calls for reform, extending the tax burden and prompting internal revolt. In short, 'Spain had in Philip's reign not lost so much in actual territory ... as in prestige, in initiative, and, above all, in her belief in herself.'[27] In spite of its partiality, Hume's work was widely read and cited, in the absence of other substantial histories of the period.

The Harvard professor Roger Bigelow Merriman (1876–1945) understood history to be an essential part of a liberal education. He was a follower of Prescott and, while he shared his Protestant sympathies, adopted a style of writing that, in accordance with Rankean precepts, allowed the evidence to speak for itself. He began his research career as a historian of Tudor England but turned his attention to the neglected history of the Spanish Empire, which became his life's work. He was one of the key historians of the early twentieth century who endeavoured to instil a sense of balance and professionalism into the historiography of the period, in accordance with on-going trends in the discipline. Merriman looked objectively at the evidence and, in contrast to Hume, proposed a non-partisan analytical assessment of it. He incorporated over a hundred years of new scholarship from Ranke's time to his own, drawn from European archives, including those of Spain. His vast corpus of material included state papers, minutes of council meetings and personal letters. In his research he quite consciously endeavoured to counter the Anglo-Saxon, Protestant bias that had shaped much of eighteenth-century historical discourse and continued to exercise an influence on nineteenth-century studies. He was a noted exponent of comparative history, as his *Six Contemporaneous Revolutions* (1937) – a forerunner of the later 'general crisis' debate – testified. He also set out his intention to broaden the traditional perspective adopted by historians on Spain's early modern fortunes. As he wrote, 'the tendency to regard Spain and the Spanish administration as synonymous with inefficiency and decadence is so common that it is a pleasure to emphasise the other side'.[28] In his carefully crafted four-volume reassessment of the structures that underpinned Spain's imperial expansion, *The Rise of the Spanish Empire in the Old World and the New* (1918–34), Merriman accounted for the events and circumstances that led to Spain's rise to imperial greatness in the sixteenth century and undertook a revisionist interpretation of its failure to sustain its pre-eminent role. Although he accepted that religious intolerance and royal absolutism had played their part, he did not consider them to be solely responsible for the fate that befell the nation. He attributed Spain's imperial decline to a series of unavoidable political and economic circumstances (including the 'accident' of discovering and inheriting empire, the difficulties inherent in maintaining and defending it, the illusory concept of wealth derived from the New World, and the foreign animosity that Spain's rise to world power generated), while also acknowledging the achievement that its imperial legacy represented. Of all Spain's overseas possessions, he argued that it was the Indies that were the principal cause of its greatness whilst it lasted, and then of its subsequent decay:

> The Spanish Empire was rather the result of a series of accidental and artificial agglomerations than of a normal and natural growth. . . . After long ages of comparative isolation, Spain was summoned to assume . . . the stupendous task of governing a world empire composed of a large number of widely scattered and heterogeneous units accidentally drawn together as a result of two fateful marriages. There can be no doubt that all the difficulties arising . . . were perpetuated and intensified by that tendency towards separatism and diversification which . . . is a distinguishing characteristic of the Iberian peoples. . . . It is but a platitude to remark that the Spanish Empire of the sixteenth century was vastly over-extended, that Spain was called upon to shoulder a burden which it was beyond her capacity to bear. But if the process of over-extension had been more gradual, the effect of it might well have been less unfortunate; it was the appalling suddenness with which world empire was thrust upon her that accounts in large measure for Spain's failure to maintain it. . . . Such widely scattered and highly diversified territories could not possibly be welded together, under an efficient imperial organization, in such a comparatively short space of time. . . . Had it not been for the monopoly which she claimed in the New World she would not have gained the position in the Old, which drew down on her the jealousy and hatred of her neighbours. . . . They [the Americas] were, after all, a *sine qua non* of its existence, and a fundamental cause of Spain's greatness while it lasted. . . . If empire can be measured by standards other than the political and economic, the Latin American lands are still a part of the picture, and the glory of having settled and civilized them belongs forever to Spain.[29]

Merriman pointed to the medieval crusading ideal that lay behind the imperial adventure as being fundamentally antiquated by the end of the sixteenth century. He accepted that essential to the identity of the Habsburg monarchy was the notion that politics and religion were inextricably one and that this mentality legitimized the great Catholic crusade which underpinned Spanish imperialism overseas, including the punishment of infidels and intolerance of heretics. However, these aims conflicted with the emergence of religious tolerance in other parts of Europe. Likewise, the imposition of imperial rule ran contrary to the principle of 'national individuality' and the modern idea of maintaining a balance of power to sustain it. Nevertheless, he exonerated Spain by inferring that 'it was rather Spain's misfortune than her fault, the result of her inheritance rather than of her own choice, that she found herself committed to these antiquated ideals'.[30] Merriman linked the decline of Spanish industry and commerce to the nation's preoccupation with managing its vast overseas empire, resulting in a 'failure to grasp any of the sound economics, which were just beginning to emerge at the end of the sixteenth century, and were subsequently to become one of the chief controlling forces of the modern world'.[31] He attributed Spain's loss of great empire builders, who had been responsible for its triumphs under Ferdinand and Isabella and Charles V, to the transference of energy and genius to other pursuits under Philip II, notably literature and the arts. Finally, he suggested that, had Spain first relinquished her imperial responsibilities in Europe before building her empire across the Atlantic, the outcomes might have been different. 'Paradoxical as it may seem, it was the very continuity of her imperial tradition that furnishes the chief explanation of the suddenness of her rise and of her fall. For her it was all or nothing; and her loyalty to the great task which Destiny had given her brought her into fatal conflict with the principles that rule the modern world.'[32]

Merriman placed Spain's fate as a colonial power in the sixteenth and seventeenth centuries firmly in the context of its past history. Spain's rise and decline was inevitable because of the circumstances that had prompted its overseas expansion in the Middle Ages, coupled with the providential, god-inspired mentality of the age, which determined that the nation's fortunes were inseparable from its political destiny. Merriman thus opened up a new phase in the historiography of the decline of Spain as it pertained to empire: one that divorced the Habsburg monarchs from individual responsibility and focused instead on the need to follow the imperial course on which it was set and whose outcomes were unavoidable.

In the early twentieth century, Spain's imperial past haunted and inspired a generation of writers to reflect critically on their plight as a nation. Spain had fallen from imperialist grandeur when imperialism was at its zenith, thus adding to its acute sense of failure and despair. For modernizers such as Costa and Ortega y Gasset, the colonial legacy set Spain a challenge to provide evidence that, despite recent setbacks, it still had untold potential for progress as a European power. For traditionalists such as Maeztu and Azorín, Spain's imperial achievement inspired a deep sense of patriotism and belief in the endurance of the spiritual bond it had with the Spanish American continent. The philosophical approach of the men of '98 contrasted with the pragmatism of an emerging new school of historians from inside and outside Spain who began to address the imperial dimension of decline through a non-partisan lens, using modern methods of historical enquiry and opening the way for greater convergence of opinion surrounding the debate.

Notes

1 Cited by H. Ramsden, *The 1898 Movement in Spain* (Manchester, 1974), p. 106.
2 A.A. Parker, 'The roots of the Spanish dilemma', *Cambridge Journal*, 6 (1953), 460–2.
3 Ángel Ganivet, *Spain: An interpretation*, translated by J.R. Carey (London, 1946), pp. 79, 115, 118–19, 128.
4 Miguel de Unamuno, *En torno al casticismo* (1895), pp. 866–9, cited by Ramsden, *The 1898 Movement in Spain*, pp. 29–30.
5 For a comparison of Ganivet and Unamuno's approach, see H. Ramsden, *The 1898 Movement in Spain*, pp. 12–39.
6 Cited in ibid., p. 34.
7 Joaquín Costa, *Oligarchía y Caciquismo* (Madrid, 1998), p. 232.
8 José Ortega y Gasset, *Invertebrate Spain*, translated by Mildred Adams (London, 1937), p. 84.
9 Ibid., pp. 84–5.
10 Richard Herr, *An Historical Essay on Modern Spain* (Berkeley and Los Angeles, CA, 1974), pp. 30–1.
11 Ortega y Gasset, *Invertebrate Spain*, p. 34.
12 Ibid., pp. 38–9.
13 Azorín, *An Hour of Spain between 1560 and 1590*, translated by Alice Raleigh (London, 1930, p. 179, 181–3.
14 Ramiro de Maeztu, *Defensa de la Hispanidad* (ed. Madrid, 2001), pp. 104–5, cited by Henry Kamen, *Imagining Spain* (New Haven, CT and London, 2008), pp. 123–4.
15 Martin Blinkhorn, 'The "Spanish problem" and the imperial myth', *Journal of Contemporary History*, 15:1 (1980), 5–25, at 16–19.
16 Carolyn P. Boyd, *Historia Patria. Politics, History and National Identity in*

Spain, 1875–1975 (Princeton, NJ, 1997), pp. 134–45.
17 Ibid., p. 122.
18 Rafael Altamira, *A History of Spanish Civilization* (London, 1930), p. 133.
19 Ibid., p. 119.
20 Ramón Menéndez Pidal, *The Spaniards in Their History*, translated by Walter Starkie (London, 1950), p. 214.
21 Ibid., p. 149.
22 Ibid., p. 167.
23 Ibid., p. 191.
24 Ibid., p. 245.
25 M.A.S. Hume, *The Spanish People. Their Origin, Growth and Influence* (London, 1901), pp. 345, 346.
26 M.A.S. Hume, 'Spain and Spanish Italy under Philip III and IV', in *The Cambridge Modern History* (Cambridge, 1934), Vol. IV, p. 655.
27 Ibid., p. 662.
28 R.B. Merriman, *The Rise of the Spanish Empire in the Old World and the New*, 4 vols (New York, 1918–34), Vol. I, p. viii.
29 Ibid., Vol. IV, pp. 671–6.
30 Ibid., p. 676.
31 Ibid.
32 Ibid., p. 680.

6

The mid-twentieth century: interdisciplinary perspectives

Historians, be geographers. Be jurists too, and sociologists, and psychologists; and do not close your eyes to the great currents of physical science. (Lucien Febvre, 'Vivre l'histoire', *Mélanges d'histoire sociale*, 3 [1943], 17)

In 1929 two French historians, Marc Bloch and Lucien Febvre, became the leaders of what has been called a 'French Historiographical Revolution', a movement which heralded a profound change in the techniques and forms of evidence employed to advance historical knowledge.[1] Bloc and Febvre founded a new journal, *Annales d'histoire économique et sociale*, renamed in 1946 as *Annales, Économies, Sociétés, Civilisations*, from which the school of *Annales* history was born. Its philosophy was essentially three-fold: firstly, it espoused a problem-oriented, analytical approach to the writing of history, rather than a traditional narrative, events-based one; secondly, it focused on the full spectrum of human experiences and did not just limit itself to the long-established fields of political, diplomatic and military history that raised the profile of the elite; and thirdly, it collaborated with other disciplines such as economics, geography and the social sciences. The *Annalistes* reacted against narrow specialization and traditional chronology and attempted to grasp 'total history' via the examination of a broad range of historical structures – evidenced in the environment, the economy and society – and so to demonstrate, in Fernand Braudel's words, 'that history can do more than study walled gardens'.[2] By adopting an interdisciplinary approach, they opened up the way to using different forms of evidence and research techniques to inform an understanding of the past. The history of the *Annales* School divides into three stages or generations: it began in the 1920s as a small movement radically opposed to conventional methods of historical enquiry and discourse; in its second phase, from 1945, it firmly established itself as a school in its own right (institutionalised as the Centres des Recherches Historiques at the École Pratique des Hautes Études), whose 'Sixth Section', led by Fernand Braudel from 1947, undertook pioneering research in the fields of quantitative, demographic, human and material studies; in its third, post-1968 phase, divisions emerged within the School, which became the subject of criticism for its neglect of the political dimension of history. The methods and approach of the *Annalistes*, a considerable number of whom specialized in early modern Spain and addressed issues pertaining to its decline, were to have a major influence on the course of Spanish historical scholarship from the mid-twentieth century, notably but not exclusively its 'Barcelona School'.

The work that served as the flagship of the *Annales* School in its second phase, and that arguably had most impact on the direction of western European historiography in the second half of the twentieth century, was *The Mediterranean and the Mediterranean World in the Age of Philip II* by Fernand Braudel (1902–85), which sealed his reputation as an international historian of the highest distinction, sustained over three decades. The book, written while he was a prisoner of war in Germany in the early 1940s and published in 1949, deals simultaneously with the history of a geographic area, a sea and the countries along its coast during a critical juncture in European history when the Mediterranean world was in the process of losing its supremacy to the Atlantic.[3] Braudel explores the reasons behind this dramatic change of fortune that had a particular impact on Spain and the power it held in the region. *The Mediterranean* underlines the importance of space in history, by making the sea the protagonist of the book and emphasizing how distance and communications (and not just within but beyond its frontiers) impacted upon it, rather than focusing on a political unit such as the Spanish Empire or an individual such as Philip II. Braudel combined his global and spatial vision of history with one that espoused its division into different temporal phases or structures. The slow-moving forces of geography and climate constituted the 'long term' structure of history (*la longue durée*), the steady cycle of socio-economic change formed its medium-length units (*la moyenne durée*) and the fleeting influence of politics and diplomacy were its short-term events (*la courte durée*).[4] The author's three-tiered model, linking time and historical determinants to produce a 'total history', was widely accepted within the French historical profession and was to have a major impact on historical studies, inspiring a whole new generation of *Annaliste* scholars, from both inside and outside France, to explore the past from radically different vantage points. Given the importance of its influence on early modern Spanish historiography and its unique interpretation of the decline phenomenon, Braudel's *Mediterranean* will be the main focus of the first part of this chapter.

The book comprises three parts. Each examines a different approach to the Mediterranean as a crucial theatre of history in the second half of the sixteenth century, when two great empires, that of Philip II of Spain and that of the Ottoman Sultan, collided and fought over it. In part one (the role of the environment), Braudel dealt with the history of man in relation to his environment, 'a history of constant repetition, of ever-recurring cycles',[5] in which he explored the geographical foundations of history or 'geo-history'. His aim was to show that geographical phenomena, as well as climatic and seasonal features, are a fundamental part of history and that it cannot be fully understood without them. In part two (collective destinies), he looked at the gradually changing history of economic, social and civilizing structures, 'the swelling currents of the Mediterranean',[6] as he described them, a context that was 'by turns favourable and unfavourable to vast political hegemonies'.[7] In part three (events, politics and people), he examined the fast-moving history of political events (*l'histoire événementielle*), which he referred to as 'the crests of foam that the tides of history carry on their backs'.[8] These, he argued, could only be understood in relation to the undercurrents or larger movements of history examined in parts one (environment) and two (structures): 'Events are the ephemera of history; they pass across its stage like fire-flies, hardly glimpsed before they settle back into darkness and as often as not into oblivion.'[9] The different components of history, Braudel informed his reader, needed to be understood as a series of causal chains interacting with one another: 'For there is no single conjuncture: we must visualize a series of overlapping histories, developing simultaneously.'[10] The historian's role was to craft and integrate its many strands.

Braudel was the first historian to subject Spain's late sixteenth-century fortunes to interdisciplinary analysis. In *The Mediterranean*, he explored a number of 'structural' features of the geographical zone, such as islands, mountains, plains, seas, coasts and boundaries, as well as natural ones, such as weather conditions, to account for the decline of the Mediterranean. He placed emphasis throughout on the contrast between the superficial splendour of Mediterranean civilization conferred by the variety in its ecology and resources and the fragility of its underlying condition that permanently threatened subsistence levels: 'In the sixteenth century it was rare for a harvest to escape in turn all the dangers that threatened it. Yields were small, and in view of the limited space devoted to cereal growing, the Mediterranean was always on the verge of famine. A few changes in temperature and a shortage of rainfall were enough to endanger human life.'[11] Braudel argued that the harshness of the natural environment and limited potential for farming, coupled with the vagaries of the climate, were to have a determining influence on Mediterranean history, obliging its people to look beyond their shores for their living, thereby fostering an 'instinctive' imperialism. 'Throughout Europe, too densely populated for its resources and no longer riding a wave of economic growth ... the trend was towards the pauperisation of considerable masses of people in desperate need of daily bread', he claimed.[12] Braudel thus espoused an 'ecological determinism' – a belief in the centrality to human history of the natural world coupled with a perception of man's fate as one of unending toil against the elements, from which he was powerless to defend himself.

Braudel also proposed 'conjunctural' explanations (relating to temporal circumstances) for the Mediterranean's incipient decline. He pointed to the rapid demographic growth of the sixteenth century, which put too great a strain on the Mediterranean's limited natural resources and consequently gave a decisive competitive edge to the wealthier economies of northern Europe, upon which it became dependent. Population growth, which had initially been a stimulus to expansion, became a crippling handicap in the second half of the sixteenth century, leading to a shortage of food and heavy reliance upon imports:

> This biological revolution was the major factor in all the other revolutions ... more important than the Turkish conquest, the discovery and colonization of America, or the imperial vocation of Spain. Had it not been for the increase in the number of men, would any of these glorious chapters ever have been written? This revolution is more important too than the 'price revolution', of which it may have been a contributory factor even before the massive arrivals of bullion from America. This increase lay behind all the triumphs and catastrophes of a century during which man was first a useful worker and then, as the century wore on, a growing burden. By 1550 the turning-point has been reached. There were too many people for comfort. Towards 1600 this overload halted expansion in new directions and with the rise in banditry, the latest social crisis whose effects were felt everywhere ... prepared the way for the bitter awakenings of the seventeenth century.[13]

According to Braudel, therefore, it was the demographic phenomenon and the secular trends associated with it, rather than the rise of the Habsburg empire or Ottoman expansion, or the impact of the overseas discoveries, that lay behind the pattern of rapid growth experienced in the Mediterranean lands which gave way to the crisis of the following century. Essentially, an expansive phase (characterized by rising prices, profit margins and populations) gave way to a depressive phase (with reverse characteristics), but this came much later than he originally envisaged. With respect to the cycles of the Mediterranean economy, according to Braudel there were in effect two sixteenth centuries. One ran roughly from 1450 to 1550 and was characterized by a general economic upswing in the region. The second sixteenth century (1550–1650) commenced with a period of stagnation during its first quarter, followed by a downturn in the 1580s and 1590s, then a short revival occurred to 1620/30 (later revised by Braudel to 1650) before the Mediterranean's final plunge and departure from centre stage, thrust out by the Atlantic and the powers at the Atlantic rim of Europe.[14]

Braudel also proposed a social dimension to the decline of the Mediterranean, related to political and economic circumstances. The growth of the economy and expansion of the population gave rise to an increase in social and geographical mobility, while the downturn in these trends led to rising social tensions and intolerance characteristic of the late sixteenth century. The nobility prospered and migrated to the towns, while the poor grew poorer and were increasingly driven to piracy and banditry. Braudel adopted the phrase 'the defection of the bourgeoisie' to describe how the middle classes abandoned commercial enterprise and adopted the values and some of the life-style of their aristocratic superiors.[15]

> A slow, powerful and deep-seated movement seems gradually to have twisted and transformed the societies of the Mediterranean between 1550 and 1600 ... There can be no doubt that society was tending to polarise into, on the one hand, a rich and vigorous nobility ... owning vast properties and, on the other, the great and growing mass of the poor and disinherited, 'caterpillars and grubs', human insects, alas too many ... Society stood on two banks facing each other: on the one side the houses of nobles, over-populated with servants; on the other *picardía*, the world of the black market, theft, debauchery, adventure, but above all poverty ... At the heart of that society lay bitter despair. Is the explanation for all this once more that the Mediterranean was proving unequal to the task of distributing goods and services, wealth and even pleasure in living? That the ancient glory and prosperity was running out as the peoples living on the shores of the sea exhausted their ultimate reserves ... Or will our repeated inquiries show the true reason to be that the whole world, the Mediterranean included, was sooner or later to enter the extraordinary depression of the seventeenth century?[16]

In contrast to other foreign historians, Braudel put forward a vigorous defence of Spain's policy towards the Jews and Moors, which he argued was determined by its evolution and destiny as a Christian civilization, rather than a deliberate strategy of religious and racial discrimination. While expressing his natural sympathy for oppressed minorities, he noted that popular pressure played its part in their persecution and was a characteristic of the self-assertion of all evolving societies:

> To call sixteenth century Spain a 'totalitarian' or racist country strikes me as unreasonable. It has some harrowing scenes to offer,

but then so do France, Germany and England, or Venice ... at the same period. ... Civilizations, like economies, have their long-term history: they are prone to mass movements, carried ... imperceptibly forward by the weight of history ... And it is the fate of civilizations to 'divide' themselves, to prune their excess growth, shedding part of their heritage as they move forward. Every civilization is the heir to its own past and must choose between the possessions bequeathed by another generation. Some things must be left behind. No civilization has been forced to inflict so much change upon itself, to 'divide' itself or rather tear itself apart so much as the Iberian civilization in the age of its greatest glory, from the time of the Catholic Kings to Philip IV. ... During the 'extended' sixteenth century, the Peninsula, in order to reintegrate itself with Europe, turned itself into the Church Militant; it shed its two unwanted religions, the Moslem and the Hebrew. It refused to become either African or Oriental in a process which in some ways resembles that of modern de-colonization. ... Political considerations alone did not determine the expulsion of heterodoxies or create the Spanish Inquisition in 1478 and the Portuguese Inquisition in 1536; there was also popular pressure, the intolerance of the masses. To our eyes, the Inquisition seems abhorrent, less for the number of victims, which was relatively small, than for the methods it employed. But were the Inquisition, the Catholic Kings, the various rulers of Spain and Portugal really the major forces responsible for a combat urged by the profound desires of the multitude? Before the nationalism of the nineteenth century, peoples felt truly united only by the bonds of religious belief; in other words by civilization. ... If the terrible Inquisition in the end claimed few victims, it was because there was little for it to get its teeth into. Spain was still subconsciously too fearful and too militant for heterodoxy to insinuate itself with ease. There was no place in Spain for Erasmianism or for the doubtful *converso* any more than for the Protestant. ... A Christian Spain was struggling to be born. ... And I prefer not to divert the debate to a moralizing level by saying that Spain was amply punished for her crimes, for the expulsion of 1492, the persecution inflicted on so many *conversos* and the angry measures taken against the Moriscos in 1609–14. Some have said that these crimes and passions cost her her glory. But the most glorious age of Spain began precisely in 1492 and lasted undimmed until Rocroi (1643) or even 1650. The punishment ... came at least forty years if not a century late. Nor can I accept that the expulsion of the Jews deprived Spain of a vigorous bourgeoisie. The truth is that a commercial bourgeoisie had never developed in Spain in the first place ... owing to the implantation there of a harmful international capitalism, that of the Genoese bankers and their equivalents. Another argument frequently heard is that the tragedy of *limpieza de sangre*, purity of blood, was to be the trial and scourge of Spain. No one would deny the trials it brought and their fearful sequels, but all western societies erected barriers in the seventeenth century, consecrated social privileges, without having the reasons attributed to Spain. Let us accept rather that all civilizations move towards their destiny, whether willingly or unwillingly. ... Spain was moving towards political unity, which could not be conceived, in the sixteenth century, as anything other than religious unity.[17]

Braudel also refuted the claims of those historians who referred to 'the odious and barbaric expulsion of the Moors from Spain' and argued that their forced eviction could not be proven as a symptom of a nation in decline. The remarkable thing was, he contended, that the culture and religion of the *Moriscos* should have been tolerated for over a hundred years. To be fully understood, it needed to be placed in relation to the whole political, social, demographic and cultural history of Spain. He explained the expulsion of the *Moriscos* in 1609 in terms of a demonstration of weakness rather than of strength: the inability of one civilization to impose itself upon another:

> Above all it was because the *Morisco* had remained inassimilable. Spain's actions were not inspired by racial hatred ... but by religious and cultural enmity. And the explosion of hatred, the expulsion, was a confession of impotence, proof that the *Morisco* after one, two or even three centuries, remained still the Moor of old, with his Moorish dress, tongue, cloistered houses and Moorish baths. He had retained them all. He had refused to accept western civilization and this was his fundamental crime. ... Even so, the *Morisco* stayed on: Moslem civilization, supported by the remnants of the *Morisco* population as well as those elements of Islam that Spain had absorbed over the centuries, did not cease to contribute to the complex civilization of the Peninsula, even after the drastic amputation of 1609–1614.[18]

Braudel had his critics. He has been accused of reducing men to inevitable defeat in their natural world through his theory of 'determinism'. Others have argued that his attempt at 'total history' was impossible to achieve within a context as big as the Mediterranean world. Braudel has also been challenged, particularly by Marxists, for a failure to integrate political history effectively within his three-tier structure. Furthermore, by focusing on long-run structural factors in historical development (such as ecology, economics and geography), Braudel has been criticized for underplaying the role of human agency and negating the historical process itself. Despite the harshness of some of his critics, Braudel's *Mediterranean* is still considered a magisterial work that changed the course of historical scholarship, as witnessed in the dramatic rise of economic, social, demographic and regional studies, born out of the *Annales* movement, that were published in the second half of the twentieth century, some of which embraced the fortunes of early modern Spain.

The work of the American professor Earl J. Hamilton (1899–1989), a pioneer in the field of economic history, in many ways complements that of Braudel and his methodology. In 1934 he published his *American Treasure and the Price Revolution in Spain, 1501–1650* – the first quantitative study into the economic foundations of Spain's decline, based on American silver imports set against increases in wages and commodity prices – which bore many of the hallmarks of the French *Annales* School, yet to make its full mark on the writing of history. Hamilton felt that some scholars had over-played the acuteness of Spain's economic decline in order to glorify their own countries' achievements. He set out to correct this imbalance and to avoid the conjecture of earlier historians:

> There has been a striking tendency to confuse the loss of Spain's political hegemony with economic stagnation ... and strong biases, pulling in different directions, have infused into economic-historical literature an exaggeration of Spanish economic decadence in the seventeenth century. The Germans have tended to magnify the extent of the collapse in order to glorify the Emperor Charles V through contrast; the French in order to exalt the economic policy of the first Bourbons; and the liberals of all countries in order to place absolutism, the Inquisition, the persecution of minorities, and the Moorish expulsion in a more unfavourable light.[19]

Although price rises had frequently been acknowledged by Spanish economic theorists in the sixteenth century as a major destabilizing factor, they deliberately avoided ascribing these to the accumulation of specie because of its special qualities (*summum bonum*) and the important contribution it made to the public revenue. Sancho de Moncada was the first seventeenth-century economist to acknowledge the influence of American treasure on prices, in his *Restauración Política de España*, observing that 'the abundance of silver and gold has caused a fall in their value ... and consequently a rise in the things that are bought with them'.[20] Nevertheless, this remained a neglected area of thorough enquiry among mercantilists in general, whose reform programme was more conducive towards changes that would increase Spain's economic output and eliminate social ills.[21] Hamilton endeavoured to undertake the necessary research, using statistical evidence drawn principally from the Indies trade repository archives in Seville to chart the relationship between the quantity of bullion imports and the impact on the cost of living and so to prove the importance of the link between the two.

Hamilton established a direct correlation between the rise in price of around 150 basic commodities (from acorns to wool) alongside the average labourer's wage (from carpenters to weavers) across four principal regions of Spain (Andalusia, New Castile, Old Castile and León and Valencia) and the amount of American bullion being registered at the Casa de Contratación (Central Trading House) in Seville. He highlighted three stages of price fluctuation. The period 1501–50 witnessed a moderate rise, 1550–1600 saw a culmination of rises and 1601–50 was marked by stagnation. His thesis presupposed a steady injection of silver into the Spanish economy and a widening circle of rising prices as the silver moved outwards from Andalusia and spread through Spain and then on to other parts of Europe, causing a 'price revolution'. If we are to take Hamilton's thesis at is face value, we might be inclined to conclude that Spain's greatness as a nation coincided with the upward trend in its wealth derived from the New World, and its eclipse with the deflation that followed, but the equation was not quite so simple. Hamilton's figures also demonstrated that wages did not keep up with price rises and that by the end of the century (1596–1600) the purchasing power of Spanish labour had declined by almost 30 per cent of its value at the beginning (1511–15). 'Thus', he argued, 'we find that the great streams of treasure from the Indies, which, according to the prevailing mercantilist philosophy, were expected to enrich Spain after the fashion of King Midas, spelled unremitting economic retrogression for wage earners.'[22] Even though Hamilton's work, undertaken at the time of the Great Depression, when monetary economics had assumed a new urgency, has been criticized and superseded,[23] his monetary theory on decline still stands as a landmark in historical method and analysis. It influenced the research of the French *Annales* scholar Pierre Channu, who worked out a model of the seventeenth-century economic crisis based on trade statistics between Spain and the New World (*Séville et l'Atlantique de 1504 à 1650*, 1955–59), as well as Spanish historians who took up quantitative history later in the century.

The *Annales* movement ostensibly seemed remote from the historiographical climate across the Pyrenees. In the aftermath of the Spanish Civil War (1936–39), Franco's Spain remained isolated intellectually and politically from developments taking place in northern and western Europe. The climate of the post-Civil war years was not conducive to historical research, least of all to research into a period of 'decadence'. At the same time, 'the foreign falsification of history' was held responsible for criticisms of Spain's failure to emerge as a modern society. The right-wing regime imposed its own official interpretation on Spain's past: one that emphasized the twin pillars of religious orthodoxy and centralized state authority as determining Spain's triumph as a nation, together with the uniqueness of its historical trajectory. The Consejo Superior de Investigaciones Científicas [Higher Council for Scientific Research], established in 1939, took responsibility for the centralization and coordination of all scientific research and its publication to ensure that it met the aims of the regime. (The first edition of the historical journal *Hispania* [1940], sponsored by the Council, included a pictorial dedication to Franco.) As a consequence of its 'National Catholic' agenda, the opportunities to engage in impartial, empirical enquiry were considerably restricted. Apart from the contributions of a few pioneering native historians, some of whose work was assessed in the previous chapter, until the 1950s political, dynastic and ideological studies, underpinned by traditional methodology, dominated the writing of Spanish history, alongside 'metaphysical' studies on the theme of 'Spanishness'. Among the latter were Américo Castro's, *España en su historia: cristianos, moros y judíos* [*Spain in its History: Christians, Moors and Jews*] (1948) and Claudio Sánchez-Albornoz's rejoinder,

España: un enigma histórico [*Spain, a historical enigma*] (1956), which prompted an international debate among Spanish intellectuals in the 1950s and 1960s. Both men were political liberals who opted for exile after the traumas of the Civil War. While they firmly disagreed on the influence of multiculturalism on Spain's development as a nation (Castro upheld the diversity of its heritage, while Sánchez-Albornoz saw it in purely orthodox terms), they concurred in their identification of certain characteristics that had isolated Spain throughout history, notably its individuality, irrationality and passionate religiosity, which had prevented it from advancing into the modern age.[24] Meanwhile, social and economic history remained largely an unexplored field. As a result, the writing of Spanish history became fossilized and out of step with the new historiographical trends and research methodologies that were shaping the rewriting of post-war European history. However, it would be wrong to assume that no advances were made in historical research and writing in Spain in the middle decades of the twentieth century; rather, it was limited in its outlook due to the official restrictions placed on interpreting and reinterpreting the past.[25]

From the 1950s onwards the breadth and scope of Spanish historiography began to develop significantly as a new, more radical school of Spanish historical scholarship emerged to challenge its traditional counterpart, influenced by the pioneering work of the French *Annales* School. It was led by Jaime Vicens Vives (1910–60), professor of Modern History at the University of Barcelona (1948) and founder of the Centro de Estudios Históricos Internacionales (1949). The period also saw the creation of two new historical journals under Vicens Vives' direction: the *Índice Histórico Español* (1953), which filled a crucial scholarly vacuum among Spanish historians, and the *Estudios de Historia Moderna* (1951), which provided an outlet for original socio-economic studies. In the inaugural issue, Vicens Vives set out what might be described as his vision or philosophy on the function of modern historical studies:

> We fundamentally believe that history is life in all its complex diversity. We therefore do not feel bound by any *a priori* limitations with regard to method, hypothesis, or conclusion. We scorn materialism for being one-sided, positivism for being artificially schematic, ideologism [*sic*] for being shallow. We hope to capture the living reality of

the past and, above all, the interests and passions of the common man.[26]

Catalan historians, primarily but not exclusively, were among those who offered intellectual and political opposition (a soft Marxist approach) to the Franco regime in the 1950s, and heralded a major turning point in historical research and the profession as a whole as Madrid, and the Consejo Superior gradually began to lose its academic hegemony to regional universities such as Barcelona, Valencia and Santiago de Compostela. What we might call the 'Barcelona School', working under Vicens Vives' direction, sought to reinterpret and demythologize the history of Spain and reorient it along more modern socio-economic lines, rejecting the providential and 'exceptionalist' interpretations upon which its official history had been built for centuries and which rendered it impervious to the broad currents of development taking place around it in Europe. Vicens Vives' views on the writing of history were paramount to this process. He was repelled by biased, rhetorical history that fell into line with the outlook of the regime and which had become a norm amongst post-war Spanish historians. He distrusted ideological history, since it lent itself to partisan interpretation of the evidence. He considered a 'revisionist' political and institutional history to be of greater value. For Vicens Vives, the writing of history should not be confined to the recounting of major events, but should penetrate through the subsoil of social and economic developments to encompass the whole human experience and the changing reality on the ground. He advocated a 'horizontal', international approach to the study of institutions and movements, rather than reliance upon the 'vertical' treatment, along national lines, that was traditional in Spanish textbooks. He firmly believed that history should interpret the facts without prejudice or prior selection to support one's point of view.[27]

The achievement of Vicens Vives is all the more remarkable when one considers that it was played out within an intellectual environment governed by rigid state censorship, opposed to any form of open, pragmatic examination of Spain's historical past. Because of his Republican sympathies, during the first decade of the Franco regime Vicens Vives was not allowed to compete on an equal footing for professorial chairs. This made him more, not less, disinclined to fall into line with the traditional direction of Spanish historiography and determined to search instead for new avenues of enquiry. During these years of exclusion from the mainstream of academia he set about publishing numerous scholarly textbooks on Spanish history, along French lines, with his own editorial press [*Editorial Teide*]. His struggle to establish the principle of objectivity in history, coupled with his own ambitions as a professional historian, led him to assume the role of an 'academic politician' in order to defend his own scholarship and promote that of others. (He was later considered as a possible political oponent to succeed Franco.) Despite his Catalan origins, Vicens Vives did not participate in regional politics and eschewed the anti-Castilian lens through which many Catalan historians had accounted for their past (as a kind of tug-of-war between the centre and the periphery). Although it is clear from his writing that he regarded Catalonia as the most advanced region of the peninsula in social and political terms, and considered it more receptive to change and outside influences than its Castilian neighbour, he viewed it as being a part of the historical entity of Spain as a whole, if one with its own special characteristics.

From the mid- to late 1950s Vicens Vives' research began to change direction, following his introduction to the aims and methodology of the new school of interdisciplinary history emanating from France and Belgium. He had been searching for new tools of interpretation and synthesis in studying early modern history and found them in the *Annales* School, now entering its heyday, with the Casa de Velázquez in Madrid facilitating exchange between French and Spanish scholars. He was particularly impressed by the emphasis they placed on socio-economic history and the collection of series of recurrent data, and especially by their use of statistics. Such innovative ideas fitted in with his definition of the study of history being about life itself, all the facets of which needed to be studied in order to gain an accurate picture of the whole process of human development. For Vicens Vives and his generation, social and economic history was particularly valuable, since it provided historians with the means to examine why their nation had not developed along European lines, using scientific evidence rather than relying on common clichés regarding its backwardness.[28] Breaking with the traditions of the past, he launched a major reorientation of historical enquiry within his 'Barcelona School' of research. He actively encouraged the collection of small series of quantifiable data from local Spanish archives so as to build an accurate historical record of the lives of ordinary people, hitherto ignored by scholars. While emphasizing the importance of socio-economic fields of enquiry based on statistics, Vicens Vives also stressed the need for history to be studied empirically in relation to religious, cultural and political phenomena.[29]

> Statistics is essential for the determination of values, fortunes, and mentalities, and that unless this is approached through a minute analysis of prices, salaries, political trends, and cultural tendencies, it is possible to understand nothing ... The historian who does not use it [statistical method] is deprived of his best working tool ... The problem to be resolved is that of integrating demographic, social, economic, and psychological techniques – based on statistics – into a totality that can be termed a 'method of the sciences of man'.[30]

The outcome of Vicens Vives' endeavours to emulate the *Annales* School was the publication of his five-volume *Historia social y económica de España y América* [*Social and economic history of Spain and America*] (1957–59), a collaborative effort on the part of fourteen Spanish historians. The composite work constituted the first general social and economic history of Spain and Spanish America to be published, with emphasis on the importance of demography, agrarian issues, land-tenure patterns, prices and wages, and the mentality of society. It was a tribute to Vicens Vives' historical vision and set the seal on his international reputation as a historian.

The trends established in Spanish historiography in the 1950s and 1960s by Vicens Vives and his followers helped to reshape the decline debate. In his *Manual de historia económica de España* of 1959, translated into English as *An Economic History of Spain* in 1969, sections of which were incorporated into an essay entitled 'The Decline of Spain in the Seventeenth Century' (1970),[31] he outlined the weakness of the Castilian economy and its ethos, dating back to the fifteenth century. He incorporated a full range of socio-economic data taken principally from the latest research by French and Spanish scholars, some of it barely published, to support his arguments, and included bibliographical information rarely cited by earlier generations of Spanish historians. In his discussion of the demographic crisis that afflicted Spain in the seventeenth century, partly derived from the work of fellow professor at Barcelona Jorge Nadal, Vicens Vives referred to regional trends and migratory movements to demonstrate variations in the pace and pattern of depopulation, drawing a distinction between natural causes and those prompted by war and expulsion. In assessing the decline of agriculture, he cited the research of Henri Lapeyre and Juan Reglà in attributing this to the loss of *Morisco* labour and revenues. Where the collapse of trade was concerned, he drew attention to the findings of Pierre Channu on shipping movements across the Atlantic. In his appraisal of the crippling effects of monetary inflation, he incorporated the statistical evidence of Earl J. Hamilton on treasure and prices, together with Ramón Carande's findings on the financial policy of the Crown. The outcome was a 'cutting edge' assessment of the causes of Spain's economic decadence.

Vicens Vives did not shrink from hard criticism of the basic flaws in Spanish economic policy contingent on its decline that continued to have a contemporary relevance: the lack of investment, skills, application and entrepreneurship to succeed in commerce or industry, underpinned by political impotence and social disintegration:

> We find no capital invested in the country either to increase the productivity of the agricultural soil or to form commercial companies to exploit the oceanic world. ... Castile's failure to comprehend the capitalist world made it impossible for her to compete with Europe. Here is the key problem in the history of Spain today. And it must be clarified, going deeper not only into the mechanics of European and colonial trade, but also into the Castilian mentality of Philip II's era. If the bourgeoisie were a transitory phenomenon in Castile, they were even more so if the industrial sector is considered. ... And because they [industries] lacked capital, technicians, and stockpiles of raw materials, they collapsed at the slightest upset caused by a cyclical crisis or by the unleashing of a new wave of inflation. ... Precisely those who did possess money petrified it in construction (churches, palaces and monasteries) or sanctified it in works of art. But none of

them succumbed to the temptation to engage in industry, or even simply in commerce. Behind this mentality one can detect not only Castilian haughtiness, but also fear of risking one's honour. ... Only later would Castile learn from experience that the wealth of a nation is the basis for a successful foreign policy, and that a sound economy compensates for a thousand lost battles.[32]

In his *Aproximación a la historia de España* (1952), translated into English in 1970 [*Approaches to the History of Spain*], Vicens Vives also outlined what he perceived to be the basic problems that underpinned the nation's history, applied to both the past and present:

Men, misery, and famine; epidemics and death; land ownership; the relations between a lord and his vassal, between a government official and the citizen subject to his jurisdiction, between an employer and a worker, between a monarch and his subject, between a priest and a believer, between one municipal government and another, between town and town, between national capital and province, between individual production and national income, between a soul and God.[33]

He considered these factors to be not so different to those experienced by neighbouring Mediterranean countries, but Spain's fundamental problem, which undermined its ability to enter the modern world, was its failure to follow the course of western civilization in terms of its economic, political and cultural progress, through the routes of capitalism, liberalism and rationalism.[34] Vicens Vives thus invited a reconsideration of Spanish history, within which Spain figured as a part of Europe and shared its evolution, a subject taken up by fellow historians, following his untimely death.

Antonio Domínguez Ortiz (1909–2003) was in many ways a Castilian disciple of Jaime Vicens Vives. He collaborated with him in the writing of the *Historia social y económica de España* and contributed to the *Índice Histórico Español*. He was in favour of innovative, non-partisan approaches to historical writing, such as those being fostered by the French *Annales* School. While pursuing a career as a school teacher, he became Spain's senior practising historian, publishing widely on early modern Spain over much of the second half of the twentieth century, to become 'the father of modern Spanish historians'. He stands out for his painstaking researches in Spanish archives (especially those of Seville and Granada), where he found socio-economic material that until then had been left aside by historians predominantly interested in political, diplomatic and institutional history, as well as other subjects unrelated to conventional historical studies, such as racial and religious exclusivity in early modern Spain, frequently cited by outsiders as an indicator of its back-wardness and a contributor to its decadence. In post-Civil War Spain, issues that touched on potential criticism of the orthodox tradition of society were still regarded as highly sensitive, and, as he revealed in an interview held in 1984, Domínguez Ortiz initially had his work in the field of purity of blood rejected for publication, for reasons that one can only assume were politically motivated.[35]

In his book on the status of Jewish converts to Christianity in the post-expulsion period, *Los conversos de origen judío después de la expulsión* [*Jewish converts to Christianity in the aftermath of the expulsion*] of 1955, Domínguez Ortiz published important documentary evidence pertaining to the statutes of purity of blood which had for centuries embodied the values of the Old Christian and defined his relationship with his multicultural past. He drew upon contemporary sources, including *arbitrista* literature and records of the Castilian Cortes, to demonstrate that there was a strong and influential body of lay and ecclesiastical opinion inside (and not solely outside) early seventeenth-century Spain that ques-tioned the exclusivity of religious policy and the justification of the methods employed to keep the peninsula free from the conta-mination of those of alien blood and creed. This led to a fundamental review of attitudes and prejudices in Spanish society, in particular those surrounding the purity of blood statutes. It revealed wide recognition of the injustice inherent in a code of practice which discriminated irrationally and was perhaps even becoming an obsolete requirement in the century after the expul-sion of the Jews from Spain. It was argued that 'Old Christians and *moriscos*, and *conversos* should all come to form one body and all be secure Christians'.[36] Clearly such a recommendation – in effect, a call for greater racial tolerance – raised fundamental questions about the whole philosophy of society upon which Spain had built its pride and reputation for 'greatness', now perceived as a 'weakness'. By extension, the arguments posed by observers cast a shadow over the Inquisition itself and its role in the persecution of religious minorities. These findings clearly represented dangerous ideas to be floating in Franco's Spain, where the Church–State alliance formed the cornerstone of a totalitarian regime, and which modelled itself on the 'success' of the reign of Ferdinand and Isabella. Domínguez Ortiz's research indirectly revealed how seventeenth-century Spaniards were more open to discussing the validity of Old Christian values that defined its national identity than were his own contemporaries.

In his *La sociedad española en el siglo xvii* [*Spanish society in the seventeenth century*], published in 1963, a study influenced by recent advances in the field of social science, Domínguez Ortiz carried out the first comprehensive survey of the two privileged estates: the aristocracy and the clergy. He proposed that the nobility were not members of a strictly exclusive or closed social group, as assumed by historians, but, rather, made up of different layers which struggled to attain social promotion and maintain their standing. Noble status, although firmly linked to Old Christian identity, was not solely dependent upon birth and blood; it could be purchased or acquired through service. Likewise, Domínguez Ortiz demonstrated that access to the ecclesiastical estate, despite its prestige, was never subject to any tight restrictions, leading both to its excessive growth and to a lack of genuine vocation within some sections, notably the regular clergy. Similarly, although the 'easy' life-style of the upper classes was admired by the masses, leading to a distortion of the values and labour ethic of society, Domínguez Ortiz demonstrated that in actual fact their wealth was much more illusory than real. In the case of the aristocracy, a considerable amount was tied up in mortgages or debts, and where the clergy was concerned it was subject to indirect taxation and the requirement to provide charitable donations. By exposing these contradictions, Domínguez Ortiz dismantled some of the myths surrounding the exclusivity of the traditional hierarchical order of Spanish society as a function of decline and opened the way for more inclusive studies.

The advent of the *Annales* School heralded an important turning point in approaches to the reading of the decline phenomenon by opening it up to multidisciplinary research and 'horizontal' methods of historical enquiry. The principal outcome was a broadening of perspectives on the debate to encompass the total landscape of human experience, free – as far as possible – from hierarchical and political bias, as well as recognition of the European configuration of decline. A further outcome, for Spanish scholarship in particular, was the beginning of the deconstruction of Spain's historical trajectory as being exceptional in nature and therefore subject to outside developments. Acknowledgement of the common incidence of decline across early modern Europe was to set the pace for comparative studies on the 'general crisis of the seventeenth century', which began to emerge in the 1950s and 1960s and soon developed into a School in its own right.

Notes

1 Peter Burke, *The French Historical Revolution. The Annales School, 1929–89* (Cambridge, 1990), pp. 2–3.
2 Fernand Braudel, *The Mediterranean and the Mediterranean World in the Age of Philip II*, 2 vols (London, 1976), Vol 1, p. 22.
3 J.K.J. Thomson, *Decline in History. The European Experience* (Oxford, 1998), p. 5.
4 Burke, *The French Historical Revolution*, pp. 41–2.
5 Braudel, *The Mediterranean and the Mediterranean World*, Vol. I, p. 20.
6 Ibid., p. 21.
7 Ibid., Vol. II, pp. 660–1.
8 Ibid., Vol. I, p. 21.
9 Ibid., Vol. II, p. 901.
10 Ibid., p. 892.
11 Ibid., Vol. I, p. 244.
12 Ibid., Vol. II, p. 743.
13 Ibid., Vol. I, p. 403.
14 Ibid., Vol. I, pp. 412, 437; Vol. II, pp. 893–6, 1240–2.
15 Thomson, *Decline in History*, pp. 13–14.
16 Braudel, Op. cit., Vol. II, pp. 755–6.
17 Ibid., pp. 823–5.
18 Ibid., pp. 796–7.
19 Earl J. Hamilton, *American Treasure and the Price Revolution in Spain, 1501–1650* (New York, reprint, 1977), p. 303–4.
20 Sancho de Moncada, *Restauración política de España*, ed. Jean Vilar (Madrid, 1974), p. 143.
21 Hamilton, *American Treasure*, pp. 290, 294–5.
22 Ibid., pp. 280–1.
23 See J. Lynch, *Spain 1516–1598: From Nation State to World Empire*, p. 177.
24 J.N. Hillgarth, 'Spanish historiography and Iberian reality', *History and*

Theory, 24:1 (1985), 23–6, 32–4; Richard Herr, *An Historical Essay on Modern Spain* (Berkeley and Los Angeles, CA, 1974), pp. 31–2.
25 Stanley G. Payne, 'Jaime Vicens Vives and the writing of Spanish history', *The Journal of Modern History*, 34:2 (1962), 119–34.
26 Ibid., 130.
27 J. Vicens Vives, *Approaches to the History of Spain*, (Berkeley, CA and London, 1970) p. vi.
28 Gonzalo Pasamar, *Apologia and Criticism. Historical Writing in Spain 1500–2000* (Bern, 2010), p. 232.
29 Payne, 'Jaime Vicens Vives', 127.
30 Vicens Vives, *Approaches*, pp. xix–xxi.
31 In C.M. Cipolla, *The Economic Decline of Empires* (London, 1970), pp. 121–67.
32 Vicens Vives, *Approaches*, pp. 98–9.
33 Ibid., p. xxiv.
34 Ibid., p. xxiii.
35 Peter Bakewell, 'An interview with Antonio Domínguez Ortiz', *The Hispanic American Historical Review*, 65:2 (1985), 193.
36 Fray Agustín Salucio, *Discurso sobre los estatutos de sangre* (1600), f. 26v (Valencia, 1975).

7

The later twentieth century: the 'general crisis' of the seventeenth century

These days are days of shaking ... and this shaking is universal: the Palatinate, Bohemia, Germania, Catalonia, Portugal, Ireland, England. (English preacher before the House of Commons, 1643, cited by H.R. Trevor-Roper, 'The general crisis of the seventeenth century', *Past and Present*, 16 [1959], 31)

Following on the success of the *Annales* School and its associated journal in breaking out of the conventional mould of historical studies and reopening early modern European history in particular to new methods of interdisciplinary analysis, further impetus was given to the twentieth-century historiographical revolution through the founding of the English journal *Past and Present*, in 1952, by a group of scholars of broad academic origins and with either Marxist or at least predominantly left-of-centre political sympathies and interests in social and economic history not dissimilar to those of the *Annalistes*. One of the declared aims of the journal was 'to widen the somewhat narrow horizon of traditional historical studies among the English-speaking public',[1] to encompass Europe and the wider world and introduce some of the engagement with historical problems that singled out contemporary French historiography. *Past and Present* soon became one of the most provocative historical journals in the English language, gaining support within the wider academic community for its cutting-edge research and lively debates. From its inception, it placed heavy emphasis on sixteenth- and seventeenth-century topics, quickening the interest of scholars in the early modern period and providing a lively forum for controversial, robust debate and assertive writing. During the 1950s and 1960s, *Past and Present* became a focal point for historians to generate comparative theories on the circumstances that gave rise to the so-called 'general crisis' experienced by late sixteenth- and seventeenth-century European states and to assess the different reactions to crisis conditional upon prevailing social, political and economic structures, as well as religious beliefs. The debate, which lasted over several decades, extended beyond the reach of *Past and Present* and became the subject of a number of edited volumes of essays, including *Crisis in Europe, 1560–1660* (1965), *The general crisis of the Seventeenth Century* (1978), *The European Crisis of the 1590s* (1985) and *The Castilian Crisis of the Seventeenth Century* (1994). The crisis phenomenon soon gained currency and generated an extensive variety of responses. Some of the resulting studies confirmed the common roots of the crisis, while others suggested diverse experiences and outcomes. They focused on a number of critical time-frames, including the 1560s, 1590s and 1640s. The outcome for historiography is that the 'general crisis' of the seventeenth century has now become a recognized period of scholarship and enquiry, alongside other key historical moments such as the Reformation and the Enlightenment.

One of the principal contributors to the debate was the Cambridge historian John Elliott, who in the 1950s pursued what was then an unfashionable research interest in early modern Spain. Through his work on the theme of decline, which grew out of his study of the regional revolt of Catalonia in 1640, Elliott sought to re-attach Spain to Europe by demonstrating that, for all its individuality, its history reflected the same broad currents of development common to other European states. What historians (especially Protestant scholars) had traditionally interpreted as weakness inherent in the Spanish national character and the shortcomings of its rulers, he placed in the context of the 'general crisis' of the seventeenth century, from which no European state emerged unscathed. He thus refocused the lens through which early modern Spanish history has been viewed by rescuing it from 'exceptionalist' and 'backward' interpretations and rendering its past susceptible to the same methods and questions posed by historians of other nations. By the end of the 1960s, Elliott had emerged as the leading British historian working in the field of sixteenth- and seventeenth-century Spain, whose intellectual stimulus generated the enthusiasm of a young generation of Anglo-American scholars to take up research projects in what was, relatively speaking, virgin territory.

One of the lesser-known contributors to the debate was the Danish historian Niels Steensgaard, who, in an essay on 'The seventeenth century crisis', originally published in 1970 and reprinted in *The general crisis of the Seventeenth Century* (1978), offered a revised critique of the crisis theory that had by then been active for fifteen years. In reviewing the literature on decline, Steengaard concluded that the term 'seventeenth-century crisis' had been employed in several interrelated senses to denote: (1) a crisis in the transition from a feudal (agrarian) economic model to capitalist forms of production; (2) a general political crisis impinging upon the relationship between the state and society, as evidenced in the contemporaneous revolts and regional disturbances affecting European monarchies in the 1640s; (3) a general economic crisis, prompted by declining demographic, agricultural, industrial and commercial trends; and (4) a crisis generated by the increase in fiscal pressures being placed on society by an absolutist state. Steensgaard highlighted a further group of historians who denied the existence of a crisis altogether or presented contrary theories.[2] These themes will be taken to map the impact of the crisis debate on Spanish decline historiography in this chapter.

Professor Eric Hobsbawm, a leading light among Marxist historians of his generation, set the whole crisis debate in motion in his essay on 'The general crisis of the European economy in the seventeenth century' (*Past and Present*, 1954), which had wide resonance within the historical profession, not least for its comparative European approach. In it he argued that the wealth created by the economic and demographic advances of the later fifteenth and sixteenth centuries was put to unproductive use in the seventeenth century by a wasteful aristocracy who invested in luxury items rather than in improved means of agricultural or industrial production, thereby preventing the 'natural' transition from a feudal to a capitalist economy. The 'general crisis' that followed, and entered its most acute phase between 1640 and 1670, resulted in tensions that provided the impetus for social revolt in the middle of the seventeenth century and was a phenomenon that embraced Europe as a whole. 'The clustering of revolutions', Hobsbawm wrote, 'has led some historians to see something like a general social-revolutionary crisis in the middle years of the century.'[3] However, the weakness of his argument lay in the fact that he did not fully determine the mechanism by which economic crisis translated into revolutionary action.

This challenge was to be taken up by the Oxford Regius Professor and Conservative supporter Hugh Trevor-Roper (1914–2003) in his seminal contribution to the crisis debate, 'The general crisis of the seventeenth century' (*Past and Present*, 1959). In it he sought an explanation for 'crisis' in the incidence of anti-monarchical 'revolutionary' revolts that shattered European states, including France, England, Spain (Catalonia), Portugal, Naples and the Netherlands in the mid-seventeenth century, an idea first posited by Roger Bigelow Merriman twenty years earlier in his essay on the *Six Contemporaneous Revolutions* (1937).[4] Trevor-Roper argued, from a non-Marxist perspective, that the cause of these disparate revolutions was rooted not in economics, as Hobsbawm proposed, but in a crisis in the political relationship between state and society. As princely courts grew, sustaining a burgeoning bureaucracy, so they infringed upon the jurisdictions previously held by the towns. In mid-century the widening divide between court and country led to Europe-wide revolutions, and the overweening central power was either brought down or rationally reorganized. In Spain, he contended, the advice of the *arbitristas* on the need to reduce the size of the Church and the State and reinvest in urban enterprise went unheeded in the face of mounting economic crisis, leading to widespread discontent that, in some instances, became mobilized into regional revolt. He contended that 'It was a crisis not of the constitution nor of the system of production, but of the State, or rather, the relationship of the State to society. Different countries found their way out of that crisis in different ways. In Spain, the *ancien régime* survived: but it survived only as a disastrous, immobile burden on an impoverished country.'[5] Such was the impact of Trevor-Roper's theory that a number of international scholars were invited to a 'general crisis' symposium in 1960 at which they passed judgement on it in relation to their own areas of expertise – among them John Elliott, who applied Trevor-Roper's arguments to the Catalan revolt of 1640.

Elliott, although he shared Trevor-Roper's non-Marxist sympathies, took issue with his political perspective on the debate. He argued that Spain spent considerably more on war and the mobilization of its armed forces in the early seventeenth century than it did on the court and bureaucracy. Catalonia, far from being burdened by a top-heavy court, was, relative to Castile, an under-taxed society with a very small bureaucracy of royal officials. Any money being squeezed out of the region was being used not to subsidize the court, as Trevor-Roper contended, but to improve its territorial defences. Yet it was in Catalonia, as well as Portugal and Naples, that revolts broke out in the 1640s. The catalyst, according to Elliott, was Olivares' plan, as first minister, to devise policies that would draw upon the resources of all the widely disparate territories of the monarchy, each with its own laws, institutions and distinctive constitutional arrangements, to meet 'the imperious demands of war'. It was the potential usurping of their regional autonomy, the shared historical experience and outlook of the Catalans, based on the notion of the homeland (*patria*), which prompted them to break with Madrid in 1640: 'Their principal purpose in rebelling was to escape the imminent threat to their national identities and to their economic resources implied in the Count Duke's demands that they should play a fuller part in the war.'[6] The defence of the *patria*, the perceived threat to the identity of the region from outside forces, including its fiscal immunity, was thus, for Elliott, critical to an understanding of the resistance mounted by communities to the demands of central government.[7]

Elliott saw the composite structure of the Habsburg monarchy, within which the existence of separate laws, traditions, economies, institutions and privileges mitigated against the development of the centralized state, as serving, paradoxically, to strengthen rather than weaken Spain's development in the early modern period and enabling it to avoid internal struggles such as those that destabilized other European nations:

> The clue to this surprising resilience [of the Spanish Empire] is to be found in the structure of the monarchy. Loosely tied together by

dynastic arrangements, it was not, as Olivares discovered to his own cost, amenable to rapid and drastic change. Essentially it relied on its own inertia – on a system of equilibrium by which Madrid, the viceroys and the local aristocracies all enjoyed a share of power. So long as the equilibrium was not unduly disturbed, there was no great movement in the provinces to make a bid for independence. Indeed, the dangers involved in any such attempt might well outweigh the benefits, as the Catalans ruefully found out for themselves after they had euphorically cut loose from Madrid. Foreign domination and social disorder were a heavy price to pay for the preservation of traditional liberties. By and large, therefore, the local elites in the different parts of the monarchy found that they could do better for themselves within the framework of the monarchy than if they struck out on their own.[8]

The French historian Roland Mousnier (1907–93), a detractor of both the *Annales* School and Marxist views on history, also took part in the 'general crisis' symposium with Elliott and shared some of his scepticism of Trevor-Roper's theory. He proposed that the mid-century revolts, based on the Fronde model, were prompted by social unrest linked to acute economic hardship. The strains imposed by the Thirty Years' War and the series of cumulative economic, subsistence and demographic crises of the century were critical to the overall context. Rather than representing a conflict between court and country, they were protests against the pressure of taxation and the old feudalist structure of society. 'In these circumstances', he argued, 'it is understandable that the struggle between royal taxes and feudal dues should have worsened, that peasants and artisans should have been more willing to listen to incitements to rid themselves of the agents of the tax-farmers, or the bailiffs with their warrants.'[9] He also observed that there was taking place at the time throughout Europe 'a great crisis of ideas and feeling, a revolution in the manner of thinking and of understanding the Universe, almost an intellectual mutation',[10] linked to the rise of rationalism, which could not be divorced from politics. For Mousnier, therefore, the seventeenth-century crisis was an over-arching phenomenon that affected all aspects of society.

Another French historian and *Annaliste*, Pierre Vilar (1906–2003), although not a contributor to the symposium itself, adopted a position more in common with that of Hobsbawm. In his pioneering essay 'Le Temps du "Quichotte"' ['The Age of Don Quixote'], published in 1956, Vilar highlighted political impotence, productive inefficiency and social decay as key symptoms of the 'general crisis' experienced throughout Europe in the sixteenth and seventeenth centuries.[11] In respect of Spain's predicament, he put forward a highly provocative set of views that focused on the notion of Spaniards being out of step with reality and living an illusory existence in much the same way as the great hero of seventeenth-century Spanish literature, Cervantes' Don Quixote. In the same way that he lived out the legend of an idealized knight of the past, so the Spanish aristocracy consumed their incomes on the outward appurtenances of grandeur, neglecting investment and disdaining labour while their debts mounted and the country slid into economic ruin. In essence, Vilar argued, 'People spent freely, imported, and lent money for interest; but little was produced. Prices and salaries soared. Parasitism prevailed and enterprise died; only poverty was left for the morrow.'[12] He underlined the nation's plight as a contradiction in terms, in similar vein to the *arbitrista* González de Cellorigo: 'Spain is rich – she is poor. She has the Indies – she is the Indies of the foreigner. She is having a feast – while her people die of starvation. She runs an empire – but she has no more men.'[13] Vilar argued that the mentality born out of Spanish imperialism and the easy acquisition of wealth that followed gave rise to a paradoxical society that failed to seize the opportunity to overthrow feudalism in favour of capitalist enterprise. Spain produced beggars and bandits instead of a dynamic middle class that could have effected such a revolutionary change in the country's fortunes.

In the year following the Trevor-Roper 'general crisis' symposium (1961), Elliott published an article in *Past and Present* entitled 'The decline of Spain', which was the first twentieth-century analysis of the theme by a British historian since the pioneering essay by the American economic historian Earl J. Hamilton on the same subject twenty-three years earlier. Drawing in part on his quantitative research into the effects of bullion imports on commodity prices (*American Treasure and the Price Revolution in Spain, 1501–1650*) of 1934, Hamilton had maintained as his principal argument that 'the illusion of prosperity created by American gold and silver in the age of mercantilism was partially responsible for the aggressive foreign policy, contempt for manual arts, vagrancy, vagabondage, luxury, and extravagance, which led to the economic decadence of the seventeenth century'.[14] While acknowledging the importance of traditional economic readings of the phenomenon such as Hamilton's, Elliott called for a fuller appraisal of the internal causes that led to Spain's decline, as opposed to external ones. In his essay, he conceded that by 1640 the Spanish Empire was on the verge of a collapse the origins of which could be traced back to the 1590s or even the 1560s, and specifically to the kingdom of Castile – the source and foundation of Spain's power in the sixteenth century – and to the severe losses it suffered in three principal areas: population, productivity and overseas wealth. In the closing decades of the sixteenth century, as the Castilian population moved from rural to urban areas in search of better livings, so the countryside was stripped of agricultural production and the crowded towns, notably in the south, were ravaged by plague, causing the monarchy's tax base to dwindle at the same time, significantly, as trade with the Indies and silver imports began to decline. There was no 'rising middle class' with the initiative to get the country back on its feet, and thus no incentive towards capitalism:

> We have, then, the spectacle of a nation which, at the end of the sixteenth century, is dependent on foreigners not only for its manufactures, but also for its food supply, while its own population goes idle, or is absorbed into economically unproductive occupations ... The nature of the economic system was such that one became a student or a monk, a beggar or a bureaucrat. There was nothing else to be. [...] The injection of new life into the Castilian economy in the early seventeenth century would have required a vigorous display of personal enterprise, a willingness and ability to invest in agrarian and industrial projects, and to make use of the most recent technical advances. None of these – neither enterprise, nor investment, nor technical knowledge – proved to be forthcoming.[15]

Thus, by the 1640s, he argued, the increased fiscal burden placed upon a much smaller demographic base, coupled with the drain of capital away from productive forms of investment and into government loans and the drop in Castilian purchasing power, owing to currency devaluations, resulted in a general downturn in

Spain's economic fortunes. Foreign bankers effectively ran the economy, at a price. At this crucial juncture, Catalonia and Portugal rose up in arms against plans to force them to contribute to the costs of war, and so began Spain's descent from political hegemony as a leading world power:

> The great crisis in the structure of the Monarchy in 1640, which led directly to the dissolution of Spanish power, must therefore be regarded as the final development of the specifically Castilian crisis of 1590–1620; ... as the logical dénouement of the economic crisis which destroyed the foundations of Castile's power, and of the psychological crisis which impelled it into its final bid for world supremacy.[16]

Elliott came to perceive the decline of Spain in terms of a changing dialogue between the centre and the periphery. By this he implied that other parts of the peninsula, especially along the periphery, suffered less than Castile from the seventeenth-century recession and may even have experienced some modest economic and demographic gains, producing a shift in the internal balance of forces over the course of the century, to Castile's detriment.[17] This was an interpretation that fell into line with that posited by Pierre Vilar (whose work was banned from publication in Spain during the Franco era on account of its left-wing tendencies and its decentralization argument) in his *Histoire de l'Espagne* (1947):

> Might not this 'decadence' be a crisis resulting from a change of equilibrium? From the fifteenth to the seventeenth centuries the central provinces had not only played a leading role, they had also a greater population and greater production, as well as economic and demographic superiority. Such a balance between the political force of the centre and its true vitality was an exceptional moment. After this remarkable success, geographical weaknesses and the heritage of the past led to a collapse which was felt over the whole country, so great that the coastal areas could not make good the losses of the fifteenth century. On the other hand, however, those areas (and the Levant in particular) suffered less from the general causes of the decadence: emigration, price rises, social *hidalguismo*, the weight of taxes and bureaucracy. Moreover, from the late sixteenth century they tended to inherit, on the Barcelona–Genoa axis, the Castile–Flanders currency flow, interrupted by the struggle against England and the Low Countries. From then onwards to the present day a new balance

of forces emerged in which population and economic prosperity favoured the periphery.[18]

In his *Imperial Spain, 1469–1716* (1963), Elliott argued that the onset of crisis, instead of being exclusively focused on the 1640s, could be dated back considerably earlier, to the 1560s, when Spain was faced with the perceived threat of Protestant heresy, the *Morisco* revolt in Granada, war in the Netherlands and the advance of the Ottoman Turk in the Mediterranean; or to the 1590s, when plague, bankruptcy, war with northern European enemies and the contraction of trade with the New World all exasperated the downturn in the nation's fortunes.[19] James Casey, a former student of Elliott's at Cambridge, took up the challenge to consider the crisis of the 1590s as pivotal to that of the seventeenth century in his article 'Spain: A Failed Transition' (1989). He referred to it as a 'fatal decade' when Castile in particular suffered acute setbacks (demographic and economic in nature) from which it never fully recovered. Spain failed to make the transition from a backward agrarian economy of feudal origin to an urbanized industrial one, approaching the capitalist model. Instead it remained frozen in time: farming became unprofitable because of high overheads (wages, taxes and debts) and industry was hampered by the lack of independent craftsmen, the restrictions of the guild system and the impediments to enterprise. Casey pointed out, crucially, that the opportunities were there to make the transition, but they were neglected:

> The crisis of the 1590s in Spain was not just a series of short-term reverses; the damage done by plague and bad harvests was slowly repaired in the seventeenth century, but the economy continued to stumble on through a succession of similar crises, a constant prey to population problems and harvest failures throughout the eighteenth and nineteenth centuries. In that sense the problems of the 1590s were never solved, only shelved. ... But Spain's peculiar failure was an inability to complete the transition to a more urbanised economy. One can identify structural weaknesses, of course: the country was one of the most barren in Europe, scantily populated, with an inferior transport system and a social structure geared to the interests of sheep-herders and warriors, which had greatness thrust upon it by the discovery of America. But to stop at this would be a caricature of reality and would ignore a healthy urban tradition with a fine stan-

dard of workmanship in textiles and steel. An opportunity was missed in the late sixteenth century, and Spaniards themselves after 1600 were prolific in their writing on the economic malaise. 'Decline' may be the wrong word to use; but a relative retardation as compared with northern Europe, a failed transition to urbanisation, there does seem to have been. The wreckage of the old without anything better to replace it – that was the real significance of the crisis in Spain.[20]

The validity of both the economic and the political foundations of the decline argument were examined by Niels Steensgaard in his 1970 article on 'The seventeenth century crisis'. He argued that the economic crisis, as reflected in trends in trade and industry, was not universal but affected different regions of Europe at different times and in different measures. However, he acknowledged that there were serious difficulties in the agricultural economy throughout Europe, linked to the demographic downturn. He took his idea a step further by claiming that if 'protection' (the cost of creating, supplying and maintaining state armies) is considered, then there was definitely no economic crisis. Rather, the crisis was one of distribution (of money, goods, services, including the transfer of income through taxation), and not one of production. Where the political crisis is concerned, Steensgaard disagreed with the 'court versus country' theory of Trevor-Roper, arguing instead that the mid-century revolts were not ideologically inspired social revolutions, as were those of the nineteenth century with which they had been erroneously compared, but reactions to the ever-increasing fiscal burden imposed by the government, which acted in an over-bearing manner through its heavy tax demands, disrupting the social balance. 'The revolts were by no means directed against a stagnating parasitism', he argued, 'but against a dynamic absolutism which, with its taxation policy, violated the customary laws and threatened to disrupt the social balance or deprive parts of the population of their livelihood.'[21] Thus he pointed to the mechanism – the authoritarian state – that related economic to political crisis. Rather than being described as (contemporaneous) 'revolutions', he suggests that the mid-century revolts be rechristened as 'reactions'. Steensgaard also called for a wider interpretation of the phenomenon of absolutism, as traditionally understood in terms of the growth in the power of the secular administration, and consideration of the effects of its regulatory policy on the formation of seventeenth-century society.

The concept of absolutism, as it pertains to the crisis debate, was re-examined by I.A.A. Thompson, another member of Elliott's school of historians, with specific reference to Castile.[22] In a series of scholarly articles, he argued that although the seventeenth-century kingdom was governed by a heavy administrative super-structure, it was not necessarily governed by an 'absolute' king. He may have exercised absolute authority, entrusted to him on behalf of his subjects and for the common good, but his actual powers were limited, subject to the contractual agreement exercised via representative institutions. The granting of the *millones* tax – an extraordinary fiscal subsidy first raised in 1590 to meet the cost of the Armada, and whose contracts were extended into the following century – by the eighteen municipalities represented in the Castilian Cortes was conditional upon certain contractual obligations being met by the monarchy. Essentially, the Cortes of Castile was able to decide the way in which the tax would be administered at local level and what it could legitimately be used for by the Crown. As Thompson has argued, 'What the establishment of a compactual relationship between the Crown and the Cortes meant, in effect, was that the Cortes, by making supply dependent upon the promised redress of grievances, expressed in the form of conditions and hence appealable to the law, had succeeded in overcoming one of the principal weaknesses that historians have attributed to them.'[23] According to Thompson, this contract with the Cortes formed part of a process of devolution and decentralization of fiscal and administrative responsibility, but not of political power, from the centre to the locality. The principal beneficiaries of this redistribution of economic authority were the towns. Local power, conducted via a series of brokerages with urban oligarchies, prevailed over central authority. Thus it was in the area of fiscal policy that the gulf between the theoretical and effective power of royal government in Castile was most exposed.

Through a detailed scrutiny of parliamentary records, Thompson demonstrated how, under Philip IV, the Crown was obliged to regularly turn to the Castilian Cortes, until its dissolution in 1664, for consent to levy extraordinary taxes to meet the enormous cost of warfare, and was required to comply with the conditions it laid down. As part of the transactional agreement, 'They [the Cortes] were able to buy off or block proposals that they regarded as inimical to the best interests of the country and of the urban gentry they represented.'[24] The amount of taxation under the control of the Cortes grew steadily, reaching some 60 per cent in the 1650s. The Crown's need for money guaranteed the survival of representative institutions. After 1665, the Cortes was no longer summoned, not because it had been destroyed by an absolutist monarch, but because a weak government did not want to risk being manipulated by it. In summary, 'Castile may have been subject to arbitrary, even tyrannical rule, but it was not the rule of an "absolute monarch"'.[25] Thus there operated an ascending theory of sovereignty and practice of government in seventeenth-century Spain that ran contrary to the descending theory proposed by the contemporary French political theorist Jean Bodin, who stated that 'the principal point of sovereign majesty and absolute power . . . consist[s] in giving laws unto the subjects in general, without their consent'.[26] According to Thompson's set of arguments, absolutism was therefore not a precipitant of 'general crisis' in the case of Spain. It was a tendency, rather than a uniform development, throughout Europe.

Divergent approaches to the crisis debate emerged during the 1970s in accordance with changes taking place in historiographical trends, as evidenced in the shift away from social and economic history, pioneered by Braudel, and towards the history of *mentalités* (attitudes and identities) pursued by his predecessors within the *Annales* movement. Such was the direction taken by the Princeton professor Theodore K. Rabb in his book *The Struggle for Stability in Early Modern Europe* (1975), in which he attempted to reassess the crisis phenomenon by setting it in a longer and wider historical perspective, relating the political and economic arguments that had hitherto characterized the debate to the intellectual and aesthetic concerns of the Baroque era. He observed a desire on the part of early seventeenth-century artists, philosophers, scientists and writers alike to be bold and assertive in the scope and breadth of their creative endeavours, as if in inverse response to the political and economic uncertainties that surrounded them. 'On every side there is evidence of a deeply felt urge ... to conquer the truth, to defeat irresolution with an onslaught of prodigious ambition, to convince by sheer temerity of reach',[27] he wrote. From the mid-1660s, he proposed, as the years of crisis passed, giving way to a period of political stability, so the strong artistic passions characteristic of the first part of the century gave way to the passivity and subdued mood of the second half: 'New structures became acceptable, aggressions subsided, and aesthetic preferences softened: in sum, the "resolution" could occur.'[28]

During the 1970s the crisis debate also attracted its dissenters. One prominent British historian of early modern Spain, known for his candid, non-conventional views, made his mark by categorically denying the existence of the whole decline phenomenon. Professor Henry Kamen turned the debate on its head in 1978 with the publication of his *Past and Present* article 'The decline of Spain: A historical myth?' The basic premise of Kamen's economic-centred argument was that Spain (comprising Castile and Aragon) never rose in the first instance, and therefore did not decline. The myth of decline, he claimed, had been invented and elaborated on by Spain's enemies over the centuries to exaggerate its weakness as a nation. 'So-called decline', he contended, 'was nothing less than the operation and persistence over an extended period of basic weakness in the Spanish economy.'[29] This interpretation, he maintained, coincided with how early modern Spanish commentators (*arbitristas*) themselves saw their fortunes:

> The word *decadencia* [decline] was with few exceptions absent from their works. They were aware rather of a change in fortunes, and a failure to achieve their aspirations. ... In brief, the picture we get from Spanish as against foreign writers is not one of precipitate decay but of lost opportunity, of frustrated potential, of a Spain which for various reasons never quite made it.[30]

Contemporaries, he maintained, were much closer to the truth than outside observers, who invented the myth of decline for their own political ends. Kamen proposed an alternative chronology to the one traditionally cited by modern historians, one that suggested that it was Spain's inheritance of empire in the sixteenth century, and the costs it bore to defend, sustain, colonize and provide for it, that instead of propelling it to greatness had spelled its ruin: 'The dawn of empire had been a false dawn; there had been no lasting benefits – in short, no "rise" of Spain.'[31] Since Spain never developed a strong economy in the first instance, the whole idea of its decline was based on a false premise: 'It is difficult to see how so underdeveloped a nation could have "declined" before ever becoming rich.'[32] He argued that 'decline' (which he perceived as a series of economic reverses) did not fall across the whole country simultaneously, but different parts of the peninsula experienced setbacks of different sorts and over different timeframes during the early modern period. Spain underwent various phases of economic dependence between the fifteenth and eighteenth centuries, affecting the wool trade, manufacturing industry and bullion imports, and these circumstances explain her nonemergence as an industrial nation. 'Early modern Spain did not have a unified economy', he contended, 'and the most useful way in which we can try to understand its evolution is to recognise that it was a backward country with poor resources, dependent on external markets and external suppliers.'[33] Kamen proposed that there were four basic flaws in the decline thesis:

> First, there has been a wholly unscientific imprecision about when so-called decline commenced and when it ended ... Secondly, wholly unrelated phenomena – plague mortality, military defeat, trade depression – have been jumbled together ... when in fact it is vital to distinguish between natural phenomena such as epidemics and structural phenomena such as economic backwardness. Thirdly, the reverses have been attributed uniquely to Spain, with little attention to the obvious international character of such developments as financial crisis, agrarian slump and trade fluctuation, so that the close dependence on that of other countries has been neglected. Fourthly, there has been regular confusion between Castile and Spain, so that despite the great care of modern scholars to make a distinction, the phrase 'decline of Spain' continues to be used.[34]

He acknowledged that there was a cycle of reverses in population, prices, trade and production located around the period 1590–1652, but 'decline' had erroneously been taken to extend over a much longer period than this, when in practice there were quantifiable signs of recovery in certain areas such as agriculture and silver imports in the second half of the century. 'The canker at the heart of Spain', he concluded, 'was something far deeper: a pattern of dependence that sapped any possibility of alternative development, and frustrated hopes of ever escaping the poverty cycle.'[35]

Fellow British historian Jonathan Israel, representing the view of traditional scholars, took issue with Kamen's radical rejection of the decline thesis and mounted a vigorous response (*Past and Present*, 1981). He pointed out that contemporary commentators were acutely aware of a sense of economic decline that permeated their literature: 'The *arbitristas* perceived the process as a recent and sudden shift or falling away from a previously flourishing condition, that is, an abrupt economic contraction that had occurred within living memory.'[36] He also questioned the starting point of 1640 that Kamen proposed for Spain's military defeat, maintaining that 'by 1629 discerning military minds were well aware of the weakness of Spanish arms in general and their inferiority to the Dutch in particular'.[37] As far as Kamen's claims of Spain's economic 'dependence' upon the foreigner were concerned, Israel pointed to the considerable industrial growth that took place in sixteenth-century Castilian towns, particularly in textiles, 'in response to the rising demand at home [...] and to the opening of new markets in the Indies, Portugal and north Africa'.[38] This situation was only abruptly reversed in the first two decades of the seventeenth century, following the rigorous expansion of the textile industry in Flanders, Holland and France. Israel referred to the fact that efforts were made under Philip IV to restrict foreign commercial activity by means of periodic embargoes. As a result, 'For several decades, the decline in textual output was at least halted and industrial life stabilized albeit at a relatively low level.'[39] The final collapse of native manufacturing industries was postponed until the 1660s. The Spanish economy, Israel argued, thus did not react solely to the demands of the international market for raw materials: it was subject to a number of complex internal variables, including changes in fiscal policy, fluctuations in demand within the domestic and colonial markets, the decline in herding, the loss of *morisco* expertise in silk-growing areas, and the power of the guilds who hampered the process of industrial modernization. Israel objected to Kamen's treatment of depopulation 'as though it were a process independent of the economic context, simply a matter of numbers shrinking away to epidemics, emigration and expulsion',[40] whereas it was a sudden phenomenon occurring in the period 1595–1621 and not a protracted one, as corroborated by contemporaries. As for Kamen's assertion that there was no agreement about the chronology of the so-called decline, Israel maintained that 'there is today a growing body of opinion which clearly discerns the beginning of [economic] decline during the early years of the reign of Philip III and the completion of the process during the middle decades of the seventeenth century'.[41] Kamen, not to be outdone, subsequently mounted a defence of his original arguments, insisting that in any discussion of Spain's seventeenth-century fortunes 'decadence' should be discarded for 'dependence'.[42]

In summary, while the 'general crisis' debate has bred a new generation of research on early modern Europe and has established the value of comparative study, it has also proved difficult to establish a common time-frame and root cause for the phenomenon that fits the historical notion of 'crisis' as a short-term period of social, economic and political turmoil that hastened longer-term structural changes in society. As the crisis debate developed, so it led historians to challenge their own theories when explored on a pan-European level. The evidence for a general depression in the seventeenth-century European economy, although universally accepted, was found to be irregular in its occurrence in time and location, as well as in the degree of its severity. The attempt to establish whether this period marked the decisive moment in the transition from a feudal socio-economic model to a capitalist one has shifted to later centuries. Arguments concerning the incidence of a general political crisis characterized by social unrest and culminating in the revolutionary upheavals that swept Europe in the 1640s have proved inconclusive. In the case of Spain, they have been challenged by counter-revolutionary theories suggesting that the regional disturbances were reactions to the fiscal demands of central government and linked to the severities of the economic climate, and not calls for an overthrow of central power.

Within the framework of the debate, the argument for Spain's seventeenth-century decline to be understood within the context of a critical period in European history was partly proved. At the same time, the deconstruction of the political and economic circumstances that gave rise to Spain's crisis and their subjection to theoretical analysis has found the Spanish model to have its own particular traits and, significantly, its own explanations and solutions. By the closing decades of the twentieth century, the crisis theory was fast becoming replaced by a new school of historical analysis that focused instead on Spain's capacity for survival and resilience in the later seventeenth century.

Notes

1 Trevor Aston (ed.), *Crisis in Europe, 1560–1660* (London, 1965), p. 3.
2 Geoffrey Parker and Lesley M. Smith (eds), *The General Crisis of the Seventeenth Century* (London, 1978), pp. 26–7.
3 Aston, *Crisis in Europe*, p. 12.
4 R.B. Merriman, *Six Contemporaneous Revolutions* (Glasgow, 1937).
5 Aston, *Crisis in Europe*, p. 95.
6 Ibid., p. 109.
7 J.H. Elliott, 'Revolution and continuity in early modern Europe', in Geoffrey Parker and Lesley M. Smith (eds), *The general crisis of the Seventeenth Century* (London, 1978), pp. 110–33.
8 J.H. Elliott, 'Monarchy and Empire (1474–1700)', in P.E. Russell (ed.), *Spain. A Companion to Spanish Studies* (London, 1973), p. 142. See also Elliott's 'A Europe of composite monarchies', *Past and Present*, 137 (1992), 48–71.
9 Aston, *Crisis in Europe*, p. 103.
10 Ibid., pp. 103–4.
11 Pierre Vilar, 'The age of Don Quixote', in Peter Earle (ed.), *Essays in European Economic History 1500–1800. Essays in Comparative History* (Oxford, 1974), p. 104.
12 Ibid., p. 105.
13 Ibid., p. 107.
14 Earl J. Hamilton, 'The decline of Spain', *Revisions in Economic History*, 7 (1937–38), 177.
15 J.H. Elliott, 'The decline of Spain', *Past and Present*, 20 (1961), 65–6.
16 Ibid., 73.
17 J.H. Elliott, *Spain and Its World, 1500–1700* (New Haven, CT and London, 1989), p. 215.
18 Pierre Vilar, *Spain: A Brief History* (Oxford, 1967), p. 47.
19 J.H. Elliott, *Imperial Spain, 1469–1716* (Harmondsworth, 1983), pp. 231–41 and 285–300.
20 James Casey, 'Spain: A failed transition', in P. Clark (ed.), *The European Crisis of the 1590s* (London, 1989), p. 224.
21 Niels Steensgaard, 'The seventeenth century crisis', in Geoffrey Parker and Lesley M. Smith (eds), *The General Crisis of the Seventeenth Century*, p. 42.
22 I.A.A. Thompson, 'Crown and Cortes in Castile, 1590–1665', *Parliaments, Estates and Representation*, 2:1 (1982), 29–45 and 'Castile', in John Miller (ed.), *Absolutism in Seventeenth-century Europe* (Basingstoke, 1990), pp. 69–98. See also Charles Jago, 'Habsburg absolutism and the Cortes of Castile', *American Historical Review*, 86 (1981), 307–26.
23 Thompson, 'Crown and Cortes in Castile, 1590–1665', 35.

24 Thompson, 'Castile', p. 82.
25 Ibid., p. 94.
26 Cited by Richard Bonney, *The European Dynastic States, 1494–1660* (Oxford, 1991), p. 325.
27 Theodore K. Rabb, *The Struggle for Stability in Early Modern Europe* (Oxford, 1975), p. 59.
28 Ibid., p. 145.
29 Henry Kamen, 'The decline of Spain: A historical myth', *Past and Present*, 81 (1978), 25.
30 Ibid., 27.
31 Ibid., 30.
32 Ibid., 35.
33 Ibid., 41.
34 Ibid., 48.
35 Ibid., 49.
36 J.I. Israel, 'Debate: The decline of Spain: A historical myth?', *Past and Present*, 91 (1981), 171.
37 Ibid., 172.
38 Ibid., 173.
39 Ibid., 177.
40 Ibid., 178.
41 Ibid., 180.
42 Henry Kamen, 'The decline of Spain: A historical myth? A Rejoinder', *Past and Present*, 91 (1981), 185.

8

The current debate: decline reappraised

> In all fields, ideologically-inspired attitudes and passionate beliefs
> have been put to one side, and a period of calm reflection and judge-
> ment ... so important where the history of the Spanish people is
> concerned, is commencing. (Joaquín Pérez Villanueva [ed.], *La
> Inquisición española. Nueva visión, nuevos horizontes* [Madrid,
> 1980], p. 6)

The end of the Franco regime in 1975 gave rise to a positive
explosion of historical research by a new generation of Spanish
scholars who, enabled by the greater accessibility of original
source materials and the opening up of intellectual dialogues,
began to examine their own past with greater objectivity and
impartiality. This new history was free from the kind of ideological bias and overt politicization that had characterized much of
nineteenth- and early twentieth-century historical scholarship
produced in Spain and that had resulted in a sharp left–right split
between progressive and traditionalist interpretations of the past.
The agonized self-reflections on 'Spanishness', a concept that so
preoccupied those historians who witnessed the loss of the last
vestiges of Spain's American empire in 1898, or who found themselves embroiled in the deep political conflict fought out in the
Spanish Civil War and were then subject to the strict censorship
imposed under the Franco regime, have now been laid to rest.
Much of what was considered conventional wisdom in Spanish
social, political and economic history has been subject to critical
re-examination over the last quarter of a century, while historical
research as a whole has benefited from the application of new
methods of quantitative analysis, similar to those employed by

French historians of the *Annales* School a generation earlier. In this way Spanish historiography is now less self-contained, and open to external trends of enquiry which have placed its historical trajectory in a broader European context. The professional writing of history is underpinned, above all, by extensive archival research and its subjection to solid, measured analysis. Rather than offering radically conflicting judgements, the current tendency among Spanish historians is to opt for a nuanced, middle-ground approach to historical problems that acknowledges the complexities of the terrain and accepts different viewpoints and outcomes. A major focus of these new initiatives in research has been the early modern period. As a result, the history of the 'rise and decline' of Spain has been fundamentally rewritten. Foreign scholars who dominated the field for much of the twentieth century, continue to play an important, but perhaps less incisive, role in forging the debate, with many of their key works now available in Spanish translation.

It is highly significant that these historiographical developments have coincided with Spain's own process of political and social democratization and its rehabilitation with the past. A substantially revised and more sophisticated interpretation of the concepts of 'decline' and 'decadence' as they pertain not just to Spain in general or even to Castile in particular, but embracing the regional identity of the nation, has emerged. The enormous acceleration in the funding, promotion and output of historical studies focused on the region, consistent with the importance attached to the autonomous community and nationalist identities in democratic Spain, has brought to light the diversity of the socio-economic experience of decline at the local level. While this has overturned the centralized perspective of history, long called for – and by Catalan historians in particular – in the view of some scholars the regionalization of research has obscured the general picture by narrowing the context of analysis. Additionally, the new historiography can be seen to reflect a heightened public interest in national and regional parliamentary traditions in post-Franco Spain, as well as the freedoms associated with constitutional monarchy and the importance attached to political membership of the European community. The shaking off of the old tags of despotism, bigotry and backwardness synonymous with Spain's decadence, forged by the Black Legend in the sixteenth century, has constituted a further aim of modern scholarship. The reappraisal of the decline debate and the nature of the emerging discourse has therefore to be placed in the context of the projection of twenty-first-century Spain as a modern, free-thinking, plural society that has successfully accomplished its transition from dictatorship to democracy and is seeking to renew its historical legacy. The seventeenth century has in many ways been 'rediscovered' as the crucible of modern Spain as the country comes to terms with its new identity and role, both on a national and an international level.[1]

Post-Franco decline discourse had tended to focus on the social and economic structures that underpinned the centralized monarchy of the Old Regime, with the aim of deconstructing the weaknesses that contributed to Spain's political demise in the seventeenth century and its failure to effect the transition to the new liberal order. Following typically French methodology, historians have examined the phenomenon via the theoretical frameworks of feudalism and the class struggle, alongside absolutism and the centralized state. However, their findings demonstrate that Spain did not always fit the Old Regime model in the way that scholars in the past might have assumed, and this has led to new interpretations being forged.

The work of modern socio-economic historians has been profoundly influenced by that of Felipe Ruiz Martín (1915–2004), who obtained the first chair in economic history to be belatedly inaugurated in Spain, in 1961, at the University of Valladolid and twelve years later acceded to same post at the Autonomous University of Madrid. Through his endeavours in the field, he transformed a subject that struggled for recognition as a legitimate field of historical enquiry in the post-Civil War period (because it did not fit with the ideologically controlled definition of history) into an accepted academic discipline, with significant repercussions for the development of decline discourse. His research owes much to the intellectual exchange he engaged in with French scholars in the 1950s, including Fernand Braudel, under whom he carried out his doctoral studies in Paris between 1953 and 1957. Although he did not directly contribute to the decline debate, the trends Felipe Ruiz Martín established in his work on population, taxation and credit procedures in the early modern period, and his dedication to solid archival investigation, inspired the work of modern scholars, who produced pioneering quantitative research and regional studies in the 1970s and 1980s and became renowned academic historians in their own right. Gonzalo Anes' *Las crisis agrarias en la España moderna* [*The agrarian crises in modern Spain*] of 1970, Ángel García Sanz's *Desarrollo y crisis del Antiguo Régimen en Castilla la Vieja. Economía y Sociedad en tierras de Segovia, 1500 a 1814* [*Development and crisis of the ancien régime in Old Castile. Economy and society in the region of Segovia, 1500–1814*] of 1977, and Bartolomé Yun Casalilla's *Sobre la transición al capitalismo en Castilla. Economía y Sociedad en Tierra de Campos (1500–1830)* [*On the transition to capitalism in Castile. Economy and society in Tierra de Campos (1500–1830)*] of 1987, stand as testimony, among other studies, to Ruiz Martín's work.

The classic hypotheses advanced by earlier generations of historians, although they have not been totally overturned and remain constant themes of current historiography, have been significantly rewritten by modern Spanish scholarship. The traditional explanations for Spain's economic failure (the promotion of protectionism versus free trade; the investment in conspicuous consumption as opposed to enterprise; the prioritization of pastoral farming above agriculture and industry; and the abandonment of labour and entrepreneurship to parasitism), around which the decline debate has been structured since it originated, have been substantially modified in favour of the concepts of decentralization, redistribution and survival. The balance between absolute government and the exercise of local rights and liberties is being subjected to new scrutiny, as is the conflict between the closed and open societies. The focus of attention is now being placed on how Spain responded to the crisis by adjusting the balance of power and resources between the state and society, the centre and the periphery, the urban and the rural environments, the overlord and the peasant, the consumer and the producer to facilitate recovery. Furthermore, on account of the wider, emancipated, vision of post-Franco historians, there is now greater recognition of the diverse sources of unity and stability within the monarchy that enabled it to successfully surmount the pressures and survive. In this respect, so they have demonstrated, Spain diverged from the way in which its western European neighbours responded to their own seventeenth-century crises. This refocusing and diffusing of the debate, aspects of which were forged by interdisciplinary and 'crisis' scholars earlier in the century, has transformed our whole perception of the decline of Spain as a phenomenon, to the extent that some historians now argue against the suitability of the term altogether.[2]

Quantitative studies in demography have figured prominently within the socio-economic framework of modern decline historiography. One of the early pioneers of demographic studies was the Catalan historian Jordi Nadal, who worked with Vicens Vives in the 1950s and whose *La población española: siglos xv a xx* [*Spanish population from the fifteenth to the twentieth centuries*] of 1966 set the pace for future scholars. The French *Annales* scholar and Toulouse professor, Bartolomé Bennassar, placed the subject in the context of decline in his *Recherches sur les grandes épidémies dans le Nord de l'Espagne à la fin du XVIe siècle* [*Investigation into the major epidemics in Old Castile at the end of the sixteenth century*], published in 1968, in which he demonstrated how patterns of death and survival highlighted social inequalities and weaknesses in the agricultural economy that underpinned the crisis. He encouraged scholars to explore the demographic decline of Spain within a broader geographical and a more precise chronological framework and to consider its causes and repercussions as a barometer of the state of the monarchy.

Using local sources of evidence, such as parish registers, tithe and tax returns, and the precision they offer for measuring trends, as well as official census data and topographical surveys made available in published form, modern historians have established a less monolithic and in some cases more differentiated view of demographic decline and its socio-economic impact on seventeenth-century Spain.[3] Although the 1590s are generally recognized as marking a watershed for Spain in terms of population losses, Spanish demographers working at local and provincial levels have revealed that the pace of recession, as measured by a fall in the number of baptisms consistent with a decline in the birth-rate, occurred gradually, affecting Old Castile in the 1590s, New Castile in the period 1600–10 and the Mediterranean seaboard between 1620 and 1630, and that from mid-century population figures slowly revived, although the pace of recovery varied between central and peripheral areas. Vicente Pérez Moreda, in his *Las crisis de mortalidad en la España interior, siglos xvi–xix* [*The mortality crises in central Spain from the sixteenth to the nineteenth centuries*] 1980, has suggested that although the cumulative losses to plague, war and emigration were of major significance, other parallel factors impacted on the history of population change in early modern Spain.[4] He and other scholars have argued that alongside the demographic depression, a geographical redistribution of the Castilian population took place in the closing decades of the sixteenth century, from north to south, as inhabitants of the once-prosperous urban centres that had sustained the commercial and manufacturing sector and its trade links with northern Europe, such as Medina del Campo, Burgos, Segovia, Toledo and Cuenca, moved to small and medium-sized communities where seigniorial jurisdiction and the local administration of tax quotas meant that they managed to escape the heavy fiscal burden borne by those living in the cities, and where there was less risk of the spread of contagious disease. Juan Gelabert, whose primary research centred on the Santiago region of Spain, has summarized the phenomenon thus:

> It is arguable, therefore, that from the later sixteenth century the population of Castile was undergoing a process of dispersal, or rather ruralisation, meaning that the chances of resistance or growth were better in the smaller centres of population. In turn, when demographic recovery came, it was to take on an overwhelmingly rural character which largely passed the urban world by.[5]

This 'resistance' of the rural areas to the crisis reversed a demographic trend that had been operative from the end of the Middle Ages right up to the sixteenth century. These migratory tendencies – a rise in ruralization and decline in urbanization – have been placed in a further context by modern historians, that of the gravitation of the population from the centre to peripheral regions, such as the Basque lands and the Aragonese territories, where local laws (*fueros*) protected it from centrally imposed edicts. García Sanz has related this phenomenon to the shape of the modern Spanish economy:

This contrast between the economic and demographic behaviour of the interior and coastal areas during the second half of the seventeenth century can be regarded as the starting point of the growing gap in economic development and wealth between the different regions of Spain. This gap continued to widen throughout the eighteenth and nineteenth centuries up to the present day, with the end result that the situation is the opposite of that which prevailed in the fifteenth and sixteenth centuries when the interior was the richest and most developed part of the country.[6]

Building upon the research of Bennassar, the findings of García Sanz, Gelabert and Pérez Moreda suggest, therefore, that this demographic reconfiguration – the breakdown of the historic symbiosis of town and country – has to be looked at on a more intricate geographical basis and understood in the wider context of the changing fiscal circumstances and socio-economic fortunes that affected early modern Spain and Castile in particular, and which were to have long-term consequences for the devolution of power and resources within its boundaries.[7]

Arguments pertaining to the failures of feudalism as a productive system have figured prominently as a theme of modern decline historiography, but, in contrast to the approaches of earlier generations of historians, they have been dealt with largely in a depoliticized context and have produced some differing outcomes. As we have seen, Marxist historians such as Hobsbawm (1954) and Vilar (1956) attributed the failure of Spain to progress from a feudal to a capitalist economy, and the implication of a 'class struggle' that underpinned it, as fundamental to Spain's decline. Until the 1970s it was widely accepted by scholars that the kingdom of Castile underwent a sharp economic contraction over the period 1580/90–1620 that was partly prompted by the failure of landowners to invest in intensive techniques of agricultural production, alongside a rise in production costs. The long-term neglect of Castilian agriculture in preference to pastoral farming, together with the short-term effects of depopulation, poor harvests and adverse weather conditions, was deemed responsible for bringing tenant farmers to their knees, leading to famine and the importation of foreign grain. However, the modern historical record has substantially modified this widely accepted interpretation. Through an analysis of tithe returns, price movements and baptismal records, Gonzalo Anes, in his *Las crisis agrarias en la España moderna* (1970), found evidence to dismiss the notion of Castile's suffering a long-term agrarian depression, maintaining instead that during the seventeenth century a diversification in types of agricultural activity took place, rather than an actual slump, leading to increased economic productivity. In the areas worst affected by depopulation, farming was intensified on 'good land' to produce maximum yields, while the least fertile land was left barren. The outcome, according to Anes, was a new, self-regulating balance between food production and the needs of the population, driven by peasant farmers themselves.[8] Enrique Llopis Agelán, writing in 1986, placed a different emphasis on the reasons for the adjustments that took place in the agrarian economy. He argued that its fortunes, rather than being dependent on the relationship between population and resources, had to be considered in the context of changes in land ownership as well as in rights to the agricultural product. Llopis Agelán pointed to the privatization of common lands (*baldíos*) that occurred from the late sixteenth century, facilitating the rise of a class of powerful local landowners (the *poderosos*), as being responsible for a serious diminution in the conditions of access to both arable and pasture land for the peasant farmer and for the long-term depression of their status and livelihood: 'The privatisation of a significant part of the municipal lands, spurred on by the considerable increases in the cost of pasturage and in municipal spending, and authorised by a state which had to resort to any means of augmenting its revenues, contributed to the decline in the basic unit of agrarian production in Castile, the small peasant farmer.'[9] This strengthening of seigniorial jurisdiction in the seventeenth century has been highlighted by Llopis Agelán and other revisionist historians as having fundamental consequences for the distribution of power and national wealth within society (implying a transfer of authority from the public to the private sphere) and reinforcing the grasp of the extracting classes on the economy, at the expense of the weak, a phenomenon referred to as 'refeudalization' or a reinforcement of aristocratic authority within the body politic. Bartolomé Yun Casalilla (1985) has countered this argument by maintaining that the aristocratic resurgence took place within the framework of the centralized state rather than independently of it and thus did not weaken or challenge its authority: '"Refeudalisation"', he wrote, 'must be understood not as a process prejudicial to the absolute power of the king, but rather as something internal to it, even though it involved the extension of seigniorial competence within the legal framework the king had established.'[10] Yun has ventured a more qualified view of the impact of refeudalization on agriculture, suggesting that the financial crisis faced by the aristocracy and the need to attract workers to their estates resulted in their agreeing more favourable terms with their vassals in certain areas, thus pointing to a greater cooperation in the relationship between landlord and farmer at local level, which benefited the peasant economy. His arguments therefore diffuse the effects of seignorialization, and the feudal system of production that it sustained, on Spain's decline.[11]

The concept of early modern Spain's constituting a 'dependent, under-developed economy', as proposed by Kamen (1978), has also been revisited by revisionist scholars, who have identified as counter-arguments the technological advances made in mining, success in ship building and the vibrancy of the textile industry. Studies of the Castilian urban economy, such as those undertaken by Alberto Marcos Martín for the commercial and financial city of Medina del Campo and José Ignacio Fortea Pérez for the manufacturing city of Córdoba,[12] demonstrate that they continued to flourish and adapt to the needs of overseas trade until the closing decades of the sixteenth century. It was not until this juncture that the availability of capital to finance commercial activity dried up and imports of foreign cloth from northern Europe began to infiltrate the Spanish market, which, despite periodic embargoes, gradually brought about the collapse of native manufacturing industries from around 1660. Notwithstanding some entrepreneurial successes, the arguments point to Spain's transition to a capitalist economy in the sixteenth and seventeenth centuries being much more limited in nature than that of countries such as Holland or England, due to fiscal, technological and organizational restraints, and not simply explained by the entrenchment of feudal structures of production.

Theories of absolutism and constitutionalism as they relate to the relationship between monarchy and subjects in early modern

Spain have also been revisited by revisionist historians in the context of the decline debate, following the identification of absolutism by crisis scholars as one of the political foundations of Spain's demise. The distinction between absolutist centre and constitutionalist periphery, as well as having deep-rooted historical precedents, lies at the very heart of the contemporary political agenda in Spain, where autonomous regional communities hold considerable sway, and it is no accident, therefore, that it should have figured as a concern of post-Franco historians. As recently as the 1970s, renowned scholars of early modern Spain, such as Antonio Domínguez Ortiz, drew a sharp contrast between Castile, where, it was claimed, for much of the Habsburg period representative institutions bowed to the financial requests of the Crown, effectively acting as rubber-stamping bodies, and the peripheral kingdoms, where institutions were able to defend their rights on account of their age-old constitutional framework and contractual relationship with the monarch. A major reassessment of the role of parliament in late sixteenth- and seventeenth-century Castile, prompted by several seminal articles published in the 1980s, has challenged this interpretation. As we have seen, 'general crisis' historians and economists have looked afresh at the balance of power between Crown, Cortes and cites where the levying of taxes was concerned, resulting in a fundamental revision of their hypothesis in respect of the absolutist state and the ineffectiveness of parliamentary redress. Spanish scholarship is now making its own mark on the related discourse.

José Ignacio Fortea Pérez, in his book *Monarquía y Cortes en la Corona de Castilla: Las ciudades ante la política fiscal de Felipe II* [*Monarchy and Cortes in the Crown of Castile: the response of towns to the fiscal policy of Philip II*] of 1990, has revised the time-frame used by Thompson (1982) and Jago (1981) in their studies (see Chapter 7) by suggesting that the introduction of the *millones* tax in 1590 marked the transformation of the Castilian Cortes from an unrepresentative body, lacking in legislative powers, incapable of challenging royal authority, to one that exercised a vigorous role in fiscal politics, reaching its height under Philip IV (1621–65). Fortea Pérez maintained that the 'contractualist' or 'compactualist' relationship of the Cortes within the state structure originated half a century earlier under Charles V, by means of a series of pacts negotiated with the cites over tax subsidies. When Philip II attempted to reform the Castilian fiscal system in the 1570s, the cities fiercely defended the autonomy they exercised in tax collection and administration within their local jurisdiction. Their victory in the negotiations that ensued was evidence, according to Fortea Pérez's thesis, that Philip II was far from being an absolute monarch who could impose taxes at will. He argued that the administration of the *millones* tax in 1590 followed in the tradition of previous subsidies, fitting within the decentralized, devolved nature of the sixteenth-century Castilian fiscal system and its dependence on a political consensus being reached between the cities and the monarch. As he concluded, 'If Philip II succeeded in increasing his tax revenues, his success did not translate into a strengthening of the state. Castilian absolutism was born with a fundamental weakness that would take a long time to overcome.'[13]

Fortea Pérez also identified the cities and their oligarchs as playing a crucial negotiating role in fiscal politics, bypassing the authority of the Cortes, whose representatives (*procuradores*) they distrusted and whom they regarded as little more than intermediaries between themselves and the Crown. Increasingly, he argued, the cities, as representatives of the *rentier* class, became the key players in negotiating new taxation grants, with a strong sense 'of their proper identity as an autonomous sphere of authority',[14] a position they consolidated following the effective dissolution of the Cortes of Castile in 1665. Alongside the rediscovery of parliamentary vitality in early modern Castile, recognition of the ability of elites at local and regional levels to influence government decisions via their involvement in complex social, political and economic networks therefore represents a further advance of revisionist discourse. As James Amelang has observed in his assessment of recent historiographical approaches to the early modern Spanish state:

> Virtually no one now dismisses the municipalities of early modern Castile as chastened and inert pawns of the central government. Rather, they are credited with wide powers, thanks above all to their deep involvement in state administration and the collection of taxes at local level. The latter authority in particular endowed them with impressive leverage when negotiating with the king, whose depen-

dence on the cooperation of the urban elites in order to sustain the royal treasury considerably reduced his own room for manoeuvre.[15]

Modern research has identified the nature of the Habsburg monarchs' relationship with their subjects in general as being pragmatic rather than autocratic, always liable to be tested against local law, custom, privilege and the devolution of power. As Ruth Mackay has noted in her study *The Limits of Royal Authority* (1999), 'Through litigation, direct appeals to the king, and invocation of privilege and precedent, and by skilfully playing one jurisdiction off against another, individuals and institutions throughout Castilian society often got their own way. They did so in a manner that ensured the survival of the structures of civil society.'[16] The decentralized nature of the monarchy, argued Mackay, did not necessarily result in a conflict between state and society, but rather in an active dialectic between them, 'a simultaneity of authority' that overrode the distinction between resistance and loyalty.

The re-reading of theories of absolutism in relation to the Habsburg monarchy by modern scholars has opened up the broader question of how the disparate elements of the Hispanic monarchy held together under the strains of war and crisis and is a question that reflects current concerns in Spanish politics over the challenge to state centralism by nationalist/separatist movements and other centrifugal forces. The relationship between the centralized power of the State and society, comprising those individuals and communities traditionally considered to be devoid of rights and power, has been taken beyond the constitutional framework of the debate. Following the lines of Elliott's theory of multiple monarchies (1992), it is now being posited that the multinational character of the monarchy itself, integrating different social and political concerns (not exclusively aristocratic, but middling and popular currents), implied the investing of a substantial degree of autonomy in elites and kinship groups located at the centre and the periphery of the imperial system, which provided an outlet through which to satisfy ambitions and thwart opposition. In essence, revisionist historians have concluded that there was much more of an accommodation of interests between the State and society in early modern Spain that transcended the boundaries of geography, social hierarchy and jurisdictional frameworks, than hitherto acknowledged. Fundamental to this relationship was a respect for diversity over the enforcement of unity. These circumstances, set within the construct of the composite monarchy, ensured the maintenance of political stability in Spain and its dependencies, outside the revolts of the 1640s, albeit under a weakened monarch.[17]

One of the potentially most contentious areas of research pertaining to the decline debate to be opened up by modern scholarship has been that relating to the Spanish Inquisition, commonly considered 'one of the interpretative touchstones of the history of early modern Spain', where for centuries the old Protestant–Catholic rivalry has characterized much of the historiography. While for Lea (1906) it was 'the official instrument of intolerance', for Menéndez y Pelayo (1880) it was the foundation of Spanish national identity. Although important inroads had been opened up by Spanish scholars writing in the 1950s and 1960s, notably Antonio Domínguez Ortiz's exploration of the status of New Christians in Old Christian society, which touched on the sensitive issue of racial prejudice, referred to in Chapter 6, it was the end of the Franco regime that witnessed a significant turning point in research into the institution. The image transmitted by Spain's political enemies regarding the practices of the Inquisition, which linked it to arbitrary justice, torture and human suffering, around which the Black Legend was then framed, began to be substantially modified through a major re-examination of the rich archival evidence bequeathed to history and its subjection to modern techniques of analysis. In 1978, a conference of Spanish scholars, aptly titled 'New vision, New horizons', organized by the conservative historian Joaquín Pérez Villanueva (1910–1994), was held at Cuenca under the auspices of the newly founded Centre for Inquisition Studies [Centro de Estudios Inquisitoriales], and heralded a new, dispassionate era in inquisitorial history. A smaller, international conference took place in Copenhagen in the same year. It revealed the outcome of a ten-year quantitative research project into 50,000 regional trial records of the Spanish Inquisition over the period 1540–1700 by the Spanish historian Jaime Contreras and the Dutch ethnographer Gustav Henningsen.[18] Their data-bank analysis of rates of repression and typology of offences of victims of the Inquisition showed the institution to be a considerably less cruel instrument of ideological control than had previously been assumed and its sphere of action to be concentrated more on minor crimes of popular ignorance than on the major incidence of religious dissidence, thus challenging some of the old accusations surrounding its activity that have defined its historical image. In 1979, the French historians Bartolomé Bennassar and Jean-Pierre Dedieu published the findings of their research that explored the inquisitorial record from social, cultural, pedagogical and anthropological perspectives within a history of *mentalités* framework.[19] The new historiography of the Spanish Inquisition has thus far, however, avoided interrogation of the institution's ideological and political foundations, concentrating instead on its spheres of jurisdiction and methods of operation, with a specific focus on its activity at regional level in relation to minority groups. While these studies have considerably expanded our knowledge of its operations, historians have tended to overlook the broader and deeper questions, as the Inquisition historian Francisco Bethencourt has recently pointed out.[20] The political function of the Inquisition in cementing the relationship between the Church and State and validating orthodox policy remains unexplored territory. Likewise, the impact of centrally imposed religious and racial values upon Spain's demise is a complex and sensitive area that few historians have ventured to approach, especially at a time when Spain is seeking to project a tolerant image of itself to the outside word. In the field of Inquisition studies, therefore, modern historiographical trends have only partly served the need to reconcile black and white interpretations of the Inquisition's role as a function of Spain's decline.

The overwhelmingly progressive themes that dominate modern historiography on Spain's decline – the redistribution of resources and the devolution of power from the centre, alongside the resilience of the monarchy and the sources of unity that enabled it to survive – while they clearly coincide with the liberal outlook of contemporary Spain and its scholarship, cannot be divorced from the commitment to archival research and the pragmatic analysis of its findings that has underpinned these trends. Nor is it the case that all Spain's 'failings' will necessarily be turned into 'successes' by revisionist historiography as it evolves in the future. The concentration of recent research on agrarian, fiscal and constitutional history has led to the neglect of other socio-political indicators of decline. The construct of the Old Regime and the hypothesis concerning its legitimacy, around which much of the decline debate by modern historians has centred, has not been totally dismantled or disproved. For all its recent profession-alization – including the expansion in the number of university chairs in history, increased collaboration between historians at national and international level via congresses and periodical publications, along with wider access to sources of research funding – Spanish historical studies as a discipline still lags consid-erably behind its European neighbours in terms of fields of exploration and application of theoretical frameworks. However, we can say that, on the basis of the current state of research, the new generation of Spanish historians has succeeded in establishing ownership of the debate and in injecting a sense of balance into their discourse.

The distinctive features of Spain's historical development in the early modern period, including the country's inheritance of a vast overseas empire, its auspicious discovery of the New World and assumption of the role of secular leader of Christendom, all contrived to create an image of a country unique among nations, chosen by God to fulfil his universal mission, and whose ascen-dancy knew no limits. When the tide of history turned and Spain's fortunes receded, its past achievements were dramatized as a series of legendary successes and its subsequent, less favourable predica-ment was perceived in equally dramatic terms as 'decline', a concept that has continued to be used by successive generations and schools of historians to the present day and has given rise to the great debate over how and why these circumstances arose. As this study has attempted to show, historians have availed them-selves of multiple theories and methods to explain the phenomenon, conditioned by their own beliefs, the preoccupa-tions of the age and on-going developments in historical studies which have built upon one another over four centuries to deter-mine the course of the rise and decline discourse. As the 'black' and 'white' ideologies that have coloured the arguments are toned down, the political sympathies are diffused and the myths are overturned by the factual record, it is becoming clear that percep-tions of greatness and weakness were less clear cut and mutually exclusive than history has taught us. Thus, we are approaching a consensus of opinion that acknowledges that, while Spain's imperial achievements raised it to great heights on the world stage, it failed to manage the political and economic repercussions and reap the benefits to its own advantage (and that of its people), and instead became dependent on foreign support to sustain its empire and finance its debts, thereby cancelling out its triumph. It is significant that these conclusions are not so far removed from those of the *arbitrista* generation writing at the beginning of the seventeenth century, and thus bring the historiographical debate full circle. There is now a common agreement that all European countries experienced highs and lows in their historical trajectories over similar time-frames and that the case of Spain was not so exceptional in this regard. There is no doubt that the debate has stimulated a rigorous exchange of knowledge on the historical phenomenon and raised our understanding both of the making of history and of our interpretation of it. The direction that the 'rise and decline' debate will take in years to come will remain, of course, in the hands of future generations of historians. At least for the present, we can say that the long history of decline is being substantially rewritten, by modern scholars for an early twenty-first-century readership, into one of survival.

Notes

1 For an overview of recent Spanish historiography see the Introduction to I.A.A. Thompson and Bartolomé Yun Casalilla (eds), *The Castilian Crisis of the Seventeenth Century* (Cambridge, 1994), pp. 1–12; James S. Amelang, 'The peculiarities of the Spaniards: Historical approaches to the early modern state', in J.S. Amelang and S. Beer (eds), *Public Power in Europe: Studies in Historical Transformations* (Pisa, 2006), pp. 39–56; J.K.J. Thomson, *Decline in History. The European Experience* (Oxford, 1998).

2 Thompson and Yun Casalilla, *The Castilian Crisis*, pp. 3, 6–7.

3 Ángel García Sanz, 'Castile 1580–1650: Economic crisis and the policy of reform', in I.A.A. Thompson and Bartolomé Yun Casalilla (eds), *The Castilian Crisis of the Seventeenth Century* (Cambridge, 1994), pp. 13–15.

4 Vicente Pérez Moreda, 'The plague in Castile at the end of the sixteenth century and its consequences', in I.A.A. Thompson and Bartolomé Yun Casalilla (eds), *The Castilian Crisis of the Seventeenth Century* (Cambridge, 1994), pp. 56–9.

5 Juan E. Gelabert, 'Urbanisation and deurbanisation in Castile, 1500–1800', in Thompson and Yun Casalilla op cit., p. 188.

6 García Sanz, 'Castile 1580–1650', p. 14.

7 Gelabert, 'Urbanisation and deurbanisation', pp. 204–5.

8 Gonzalo Anés, 'The agrarian "depression", in Castile in the seventeenth

century', in Thompson and Yun Casalilla op cit., pp. 73–6.

9 Enrique Llopis Agelán, 'Castilian agriculture in the seventeenth century: Depression or "readjustment and adaptation"?', in Thompson and Yun Casalilla op cit., p. 94.

10 Bartolomé Yun Casalilla, 'The Castilian aristocracy in the seventeenth century: Crisis, refeudalisation, or political offensive?', in Thompson and Yun Casalilla op cit., p. 285.

11 Barolomé Yun Casalilla, 'Spain and the seventeenth-century crisis: Some final considerations', in Thompson and Yun Casalilla op cit., p. 318.

12 Alberto Marcos Martín, *Auge de declive de un núcleo mercantile y financiero de Castilla la Vieja: Evolución demográfica de Medina del Campo en los siglos XVI y XVII* (Valladolid, 1978); José Ignacio Fortea Pérez, *Córdoba en el siglo XVI: las bases demográficas y económicas de una expansión urbana* (Córdoba, 1981).

13 José Ignacio Fortea Pérez, *Monarquía y Cortes en la Corona de Castilla: Las Ciudades ante la Política Fiscal de Felipe II* (Salamanca, 1990), p. 516.

14 Ibid., p. 403.

15 Amelang, 'The peculiarities of the Spaniards', p. 42.

16 Ruth Mackay, *The Limits of Royal Authority. Resistance and Obedience in Seventeenth-Century Castile* (Cambridge, 1999), p. 13.

17 Amelang, 'The peculiarities of the Spaniards', pp. 43–7.

18 Jaime Contreras and Gustave Henningsen, 'Forty-four thousand cases of the Spanish Inquisition (1540–1700): Analysis of a Historical Data Bank', in Gustav Henningsen and John Tedeschi (eds), *The Inquisition in Early Modern Europe: Sources and Methods* (Dekalb, IL, 1986), pp. 100–29.

19 Bartolomé Bennassar (ed.), *L'Inquisition Espagnole, xve–xixe siècles* (Paris, 1979).

20 Francisco Bethencourt, *The Inquisition. A Global History, 1478–1834*, trans. by Jean Birrell (Cambridge, 2009), pp. 1–3.

FURTHER READING

The following is a guide to reading beyond the key works of decline historians examined in each chapter. For the benefit of non-Spanish readers, the majority of texts are in English.

General

Carolyn P. Boyd, *Historia Patria. Politics, History and National Identity in Spain, 1875–1975* (Princeton, NJ, 1997).

J.N. Hillgarth, *The Mirror of Spain, 1500–1700. The Formation of a Myth* (Ann Arbor, MI, 2003)

Henry Kamen, *Imagining Spain. Historical Myth and National Identity* (New Haven, CT and London, 2008).

Gonzalo Pasamar, *Apologia and Criticism. Historians and the History of Spain, 1500–2000* (Bern, 2010).

Gonzalo Pasamar and Ignacio Peiró, *Diccionario Akal de historiadores españoles contemporáneos (1840–1980)* (Madrid, 2002).

The sixteenth century: the Black Legend

Ricardo García Cárcel, *La leyenda negra. Historia y opinión* (Madrid, 1992).

Charles Gibson, *The Black Legend: Anti-Spanish Attitudes in the Old World and the New* (New York, 1971).

Julián Juderías, *La Leyenda Negra: Estudios acerca del concepto de España en el extranjero* (1914; reprint Madrid, 2007).

William S. Maltby, *The Black Legend in England: the Development of anti-Spanish Sentiment, 1558–1660* (Durham, NC, 1971).

Margaret Rich Greer (ed.), *Rereading the Black Legend* (Chicago, IL and London, 2008).

The seventeenth century: *Arbitrismo* and decline

Robert Bireley, *The Counter-Reformation Prince. Anti-Machiavellianism or Catholic Statecraft in Early Modern Europe* (Chapel Hill, NC and London, 1990).

Peter Burke, 'Tradition and experience: The idea of decline from Bruni to Gibbon', *Daedalus*, 105 (1976), 137–52.

Anne J. Cruz, *Discourses of Poverty: Social Reform and the Picaresque Novel in Early Modern Spain* (Toronto, 1999).

J.H. Elliott, 'Self-perception and decline in early seventeenth-century Spain', *Past and Present*, 74 (1977), 41–61.

J.A. Fernández Santamaría, *Reason of State and Statecraft in Spanish Political Thought, 1595–1640* (Boston, MA, 1983).

Michael D. Gordon, 'Morality, reform and the Empire in seventeenth-century Spain', *Il Pensiero Político*, 11 (1978), 3–19.

Marjorie Grice-Hutchinson, *Early Economic Thought in Spain, 1177–1740* (London, 1978).

Jean Vilar, *Literatura y Economía: La figura satírica del arbitrista en el siglo de oro* (Madrid, 1973).

The eighteenth century: enlightened opinion

Jorge Cañizares-Esguerra, 'Eighteenth-century Spanish political economy: Epistemology and decline', *Eighteenth-Century Thought*, 1 (2003), 295–314.

Richard Herr, *The Eighteenth Century Revolution in Spain* (Princeton, NJ, 1958).

María Carmen Iglesias, 'Montesquieu and Spain: Iberian identity as seen through the eyes of a non-Spaniard of the eighteenth-century', in Richard Herr and John H.R. Polt (eds), *Iberian Identity. Essays on the Nature of Identity in Portugal and Spain* (Berkeley, CA, 1998), pp. 143–55.

Paul Ilie, 'Exomorphism: Cultural bias and the French image of Spain from the War of Succession to the age of Voltaire', *Eighteenth-Century Studies*, 9 (Spring, 1976), 375–89.

Chales Jago, 'The eighteenth century economic analysis of the decline of Spain', in Paul Fritz and David Williams (eds), *The Triumph of Culture: Eighteenth Century Perspectives* (Toronto, 1972), pp. 335–52.

John Lynch, *Bourbon Spain, 1700–1808* (Oxford, 1989).

Ruth MacKay, *Lazy, Improvident People. Myth and Reality in the Writing of Spanish History* (Ithaca, NY and London, 2006).

The nineteenth century: liberalism and conservatism

Douglas W. Foard, 'The Spanish Fichte: Menéndez y Pelayo', *Journal of Contemporary History*, 14:1 (1979), 83–97.

Stephen Haliczer, 'Inquisition myth and Inquisition history: The abolition of the Holy Office and the development of Spanish political ideology', in A. Alcalá (ed.), *The Spanish Inquisition and the Inquisitorial Mind* (Boulder, CO, 1987), pp. 523–46.

Richard L. Kagan, 'Prescott's paradigm: American historical scholarship and the decline of Spain', *The American Historical Review*, 101:2 (1996), 423–46.

John Lynch, 'Menéndez Pelayo as a historian', *Bulletin of Spanish Studies*, 33:4 (1956), 187–201.

John M. O'Brien, 'Henry Charles Lea: The historian as reformer', *American Quarterly*, 19:1 (1967), 104–13.

Edward Peters, 'Henry Charles Lea and the abode of monsters', in A. Alcalá (ed.), *The Spanish Inquisition and the Inquisitorial Mind* (Boulder, CO, 1987), pp. 577–608.

George L. Vásquez, 'Cánovas and the decline of Spain', *Mediterranean Historical Review*, 7:1 (1992), 66–91.

The early twentieth century: imperialism and decline

Martin Blinkhorn, 'The "Spanish problem" and the imperial myth', *Journal of Contemporary History*, 15:1 (1980), 5–25.

John E. Fagg, 'Rafael Altamira', in S. William Halperin (ed.), *Essays in Modern European Historiography* (Chicago, IL and London, 1970), pp. 3–21.

Thomas Matthews, 'Rafael Altamira: An appreciation', *The Hispanic American Historical Review*, 32:3 (1952), 452–7.

H. Ramsden, *The 1898 Movement in Spain* (Manchester, 1974).

Colin Smith, 'Ramón Menéndez Pidal, 1869–1968', *Diamante*, 19 (London: The Hispanic and Lugo Brazilian Councils, 1970), 1–30.

Walter Starkie (ed.), Introduction to Ramón Menéndez Pidal, *The Spaniards in Their History* (London, 1950).

The mid-twentieth century: interdisciplinary perspectives

Peter Bakewell, 'An interview with Antonio Domínguez Ortiz', *The Hispanic American Historical Review*, 65:2 (1985), 189–202.

Peter Burke, *The French Historical Revolution. The Annales School, 1929–89* (Cambridge, 1990).

J.N. Hillgarth, 'Spanish historiography and Iberian reality', *History and Theory*, 24:1 (1985), 23–43.

Gabriel Jackson, 'The historical writing of Jaime Vicens Vives', *The American Historical Review*, 75:3 (1970), 808–15.

Stanley G. Payne, 'Jaime Vicens Vives and the writing of Spanish history', *The Journal of Modern History*, 34:2 (1962), 119–34.

The later twentieth century: the general crisis of the seventeenth century

Trevor Aston (ed.), *Crisis in Europe, 1560–1660* (London, 1965).

Peter Clark (ed.), *The European Crisis of the 1590s* (London, 1985).

J.H. Elliott, *Spain and Its World, 1500–1700* (New Haven, CT and London, 1989).

Geoffrey Parker and Lesley M. Smith (eds), *The general crisis of the Seventeenth Century* (London, 1978).

Randolph Starn, 'Historians and "crisis"', *Past and Present*, 52 (1971), 3–22.

J.K.J. Thomson, *Decline in History. The European Experience* (Oxford, 1998).

The current debate: decline reappraised

James S. Amelang, 'The peculiarities of the Spaniards: Historical approaches to the early modern state', in J.S. Amelang and S. Beer (eds), *Public Power in Europe: Studies in Historical Transformations* (Pisa, 2006), pp. 39–56.

Andrés Antonlín Hofrichter, 'Spanish history of historiography: Recent developments', *History Compass*, 8:7 (2010), 668–81.

FURTHER READING

Pedro Ruiz Torres, 'Political uses of the history of Spain', *Mediterranean Historical Review*, 16:1 (2001), 95–116.

I.A.A. Thompson and Bartolomé Yun Casalilla (eds), *The Castilian Crisis of the Seventeenth Century* (Cambridge, 1994).

INDEX

Numbers in italics refer to figures.

Rise and decline phenomenon 1–2, 165–6
Rodríguez de Campomanes, Pedro (1723–1802)
Economic Societies of Friends of the Nation 60–1
Influence of arbitristas 61
Labour ethic 60
Land ownership 59
Liberal economics 61–2
Origins 58–9
Role of history 60–1
Roman Empire 33
Royal Academy of History 60, 63, 78
Ruiz Martín, Felipe (1915–2004)
Influence on historical discourse 153–4

Saavedra Fajardo, Diego (1584–1648) 32
Agricultural decay 46
Christian statecraft 46
Clerical estate 47
Labour ethic 47
New World wealth 46
Taxation policy 47
Salamanca School 35
Sánchez Albornoz, Claudio (1893–1984) 121–2
Smith, Adam (1723–90) 62
Spanish American colonies: loss (1898) 6, 91–2
Spanish Civil War (1936–39) 4, 6, 76, 100, 122, 151, 153
Spanish Inquisition
Criticism 22–3, 24–5, 27, 53–4, 69–72
Defence 77–8, 80, 163
Revisionist interpretations 86–8, 163–4

Spanishness (see Hispanidad)
Steensgaard, Niels
General Crisis theories 134
Political crisis 142–3

Thompson, I.A.A.
Absolutism vs constitutionalsim 143–4, 160
Trade see Mercantilism
Trevor-Roper, Hugh (1914–2003)
State vs society theory 135–6, 137
Two Spains 3, 29, 35, 75, 81

Unamuno, Miguel de (1864–1936)
Europeanisation of Spain 94–5

Vicens Vives, Jaime (1910–60)
Barcelona School 123
Historical philosophy 122–4
Influence of Annales School 124–5
Socio-economic histories 125–7
Victoria, Francisco de (c.1492–1546) 14
Vilar, Pierre (1806–2003)
Centre and periphery 140–1
Paradoxical society 137–8
Voltaire (Francois-Marie Arouet) (1694–1778)
Spanish Inquisition: critique 53–4

War of Independence (1808–14) 8, 68, 69
White Legend 5, 29, 79

Yun Casalilla, Bartolomé
Refeudalisation 158–9